The Re-Wilding of Womxn

Release Your Inner Wild to Live the Life of Your Dreams

www.powderriverpublishing.com

Reviews

"I LOVE IT. The book I wish I could have read years ago. Brutally honest, this book will likely make you go "oh.. it me" numerous times. But it also gives you strategies to deal with those realizations, and ways to find your inner wild, grow it, and even grow up. From crazy trauma to learning to ride motorcycles, the author nails it, and brings her stories to life through words, words that will resonate with every womxn out there."

Savannah Rose
Curator, Maiden Moto Art Show
@themouseandthemoto

"Life's greatest challenge is we must author a story that makes sense, belongs to us, that we can fully live into. Life takes us in many directions, sometimes away from our true selves. Plot twist -- time to re-author our own role in our story! The Re-Wilding is a powerful, personal journey to help us see how we might rediscover who we are when we feel like we have been betrayed, or like we betrayed ourselves. Join Aimee on her quest to help us return home to our own bodies and minds. Open road! Wind to our knees! Free again!"

Elizabeth A. Roumell, Ph.D.
Associate Professor at Texas A&M, Researcher, Writer, Wild-ish

"As a female entrepreneur who is passionate about helping other women grow their dreams into successful businesses, I appreciate Dr. Aimee's guidance on Re-Wilding your career. As women, it is long overdue we reshape our careers on our own terms to experience greater success in all areas of our lives!"

Casey Kuckert
Business Coach & Six Figure Women's Mastermind

"The Re-Wilding of Womxn" offers readers a chance to birth the rebel within each of us- minus the labor pains. Dr. Aimee offers simple, practical suggestions on how to transform from an unfulfilled life giving only to societal expectations to the WILD WOMXN we were all created to be. "

Christal Fields
Mother & Motorcycle Experiential Ride Director
@ThatGirl_Gogo

Aimee is a woman after my own heart. This book will be such a revelation to all women getting in touch with her inner wild so she can apply it to all facets of her life!

Kimba Reams
MSF Certified Rider Coach, Revzilla Rider
Kimba The Lioness, LLC - Owner @kimba_the_lioness

Published by:
Powder River Publishing LLC
1014 Black Mountain Road
Thermopolis, Wyoming 82443

Copyright © 2022
ISBN: 978-1-956881-12-7
Printed in the United States of America

No part of this publication may be reproduced, stored, transmitted in any form — electronic, mechanical, digital photocopy, recording, or other without the express written approval of the author.

All rights reserved solely by the author. The author guarantees all are original and do not infringe upon the legal right of any other person or work. The views expressed in this book are not necessarily that of the publisher.

All photography was used with the permission of the photographers and cannot be used, or reproduced without the express written permission of the photographer.

Table of Contents

Preface — 1

Chapter 1 — 4

Chapter 2 — 16

Chapter 3 — 25

Chapter 4 — 37

Chapter 5 — 54

Chapter 6 — 65

Chapter 7 — 84

Chapter 8 — 99

Chapter 9 — 112

C hapter 10 — 125

Chapter 11 — 145

Epilogue — 153

Preface

"It actually doesn't take much to be considered a difficult woman. That's why there are so many of us." **Jane Goodall**

Marilyn Monroe was much more than a pretty face and the dumb blonde Hollywood made her out to be. She was a strong female force during her time on this earth. Her radiant images still capture our hearts today. Marilyn had something powerful inside of her she called her "sun energy." One sunny afternoon, as Marilyn was walking through Times Square, not one person noticed who she was. She turned and looked at her friend and said, "Watch this." Moments later, she was swarmed by fans. Marilyn explained this is what happens when she turns on her sun energy. She was fully aware of the power inside of her and how to use it as an indomitable force.

You also have this amazing power inside of you. What Marilyn called her sun energy, we will refer to as your inner wild throughout this book. Your inner wild is alive inside of you and you can use it to attract positive change in your life. Even when life distracts you from your inner wild, it is always there, burning like a pilot light that never goes out.

Are you a woman who finds herself at the intersection of...
Wild and wise
Direct & loving
Acknowledging & healing
Deep pain & deep self-love
Breakdown & breakthrough?
Then re-wilding is for you.

Toni Morrison said, "If there's a book that you want to read, but it hasn't been written yet, then you must write it," so that's what I did. I wish I could have read this book 20 years ago. As a woman tiptoeing along the balance beam of doing what I "should" do in society versus being true to myself, I have been in desperate need of this book my entire life.

    This book is long overdue for women. It contains an expansion of every conversation I have with my best friends who struggle with self-love and successfully negotiating their identities in this world to live their best lives. Sometimes, especially as women, we just need a nurturing reminder of how powerful we truly are when we connect with the most beautiful parts of ourselves. Half of my life I have experienced the domesticating influences of society due to my gender, and the other half of my life I have spent tearing down the invisible prison bars built around me based upon how society thinks I should live my life because I'm a woman. I am here to remind you "well behaved women rarely make history" and your inner wild is here to help you experience greater inner peace on the inside and success on the outside. Your inner wild has a rightful place in the world, and she deserves to be set free.

    We recently witnessed the awesome power of the #MeToo movement. The #MeToo movement is a dynamic example of re-wilding. Finally, women felt safe and empowered enough to come forward united in courage to expose the many ways they were taken advantage of by men who abused their power in despicable ways. For the first time in decades, we saw women revolutionize and refuse to put up with anymore bullshit. They collectively took back ownership of their identities transforming them from victims to powerful survivors. As women we need to continue this momentum of progressing forward in society as an unbreakable sisterhood of support and solidarity.

    We have come a long way, but we still have a long way to go. Womxn deserve to reunite with their true inner wild child to manifest the life of their dreams on their own terms. Babes, It's time for the #MeNext Revolution

    We are going to get wild. We are going to talk about sex. You are going to learn to love the delicious body you are in. You are going to learn to ditch your inner mean girl to experience more intimacy with yourself and your lover(s). You will learn how to connect and manifest your inner wild through breathwork, meditation, and self-reflection exercises. You are also going to learn how to put your inner wild to work for you and be a boss babe. When I chose to live life on my own terms, I experienced greater happiness and success in my life, work, and relationships. I will help you to do the same. We will set out on a journey together to rediscover your inner wild. It is ok to live life on your own terms and not live your life the way society tells you to. It is possible to re-wild and find yourself experiencing greater happiness and success, not to mention increased spiritual and physical wellbeing. You deserve to live your very best life!

Author's Note on Chapter Two

It took me over a decade to heal enough to write my story. The first half of Chapter Two shares a story of extreme violence and survival. After having some of my close friends read this section of the book it retriggered their past trauma and became a highly emotional experience for them. I would like to offer a hall pass to please skip this section of the book if you feel triggered by accounts of domestic violence and abuse. I am grateful for the healing and even more grateful for being able to share this story as I truly hope it can help others in any way possible.

I just want to add, my heart truly goes out to our veterans. They experience intense life or death trauma for months, even years, on end while deployed and in combat. I am so grateful there is more exposure and less stigma associated with having PTSD for our warriors. I pray we can continue to do better to help them heal. That is one way we truly can thank them for their selfless service.

Re-Wilding Safely

Because re-wilding often helps us feel empowered, this must be said. There are other major shifts that can happen when we re-wild, such as leaving an abusive relationship, that can put your safety at risk. The process of re-wilding is not meant to put you in danger. If you find yourself in this situation, please know you are not alone. You are loved and your life has value! Please proceed with help and extreme caution. I include resources at the end of this book to help in these situations. Leaving an abusive partner is complex and dangerous. According to the Domestic Abuse Shelter, Inc., "of the total domestic violence homicides, about 75% of the victims are killed as they attempt to leave the relationship."

Please don't do it alone and please do not put your safety (or your children) at risk. You CAN leave and you can do so safely. I have been there and understand your fear. I have also lost two girlfriends to abusers who murdered them when they decided to leave. Their lives were so precious. Please take care of yourself.
There are incredible organizations out there that can help you (and your children) transition from a dangerous situation to a safe place.

Why Does He Do That: Inside the Minds of Angry and Controlling Men, by Lundy Bancroft, is a book that safe shelters often give to women stuck in the vicious cycle of abuse. Lundy is a therapist who has spent his entire career working with abusive men. I have read his book and I was shocked to discover that it is a fact that the vast majority of abusers don't change. His book is straightforward and helps women recognize when they are being controlled and abused and lists ways to safely exit an abusive relationship. Help is available. The number to the Domestic Violence Hotline is 1-800-799-7233.

If you find you are in a dangerous situation, please know you are loved and re-wild safely.

Don't Go Changing

I didn't write this book to change you. I wrote this book to remind you that you are fucking wild and unstoppable. The purpose of this book is to inspire and empower you to reconnect with your true inner "wild" self. You deserve to experience and manifest self-love and brave wellbeing to live your best life on your own terms.

Re-Wilding is the best thing that can happen to you. Your life will never be the same.

Let's get started.

Chapter 1: Baby, You Were Born Wild

Once upon a time there was a little girl born wild and free. As a baby she was adored and coddled by her family and all who met her. As a little girl her father called her "princess." Every time she cried her mom or dad would immediately hold her to comfort her. They would do anything to make sure she felt better. The little girl thought it was odd that when she cried, she got so much attention, but when her brother cried, her daddy told him to "stop crying and be a man." She never understood why she was held and rocked until her tears dried up, but her brother was not allowed to cry.

She saw this happen at her friends' houses too. Why weren't brothers allowed to cry? She wondered if little boys even cried at all. If they did cry, they must have done it all alone in a hiding place. The little girl realized little boys and girls were treated differently. Soon the little girl joined in the crowd of neighborhood kids who made fun of little boys when they cried.

The little girl quickly realized she could even cry to get what she wanted. Her big brother annoyed her all the time. In the spirit of sibling rivalry, when she wanted to get him in trouble, she would fake cry and tell her parents "He hit me." At first, that tactic worked every time and she couldn't help but flash a devilish grin at her brother. "Ha-ha! I got you back!" Eventually the little girl's parents figured out she was full of shit.

All the boys in the neighborhood had cool toys. They had toys that you could put together. Boy toys did cool things. Why didn't she get fun toys like the boys? They had the coolest bikes and one boy who lived next door even had a racetrack that had remote control fast cars that zoomed around and around. Her dolls just sat there. If you pushed a button they would cry. How annoying, she thought. She got bored of holding a lifeless, plastic doll all day. She even had the newest doll everyone thought all little girls wanted. If you poured water in the doll, she peed. She had zero interest in that whiny, leaky piece of plastic.

She did not understand why it was automatically assumed she would love dolls just because she was a girl. Dolls were boring. And why were they all white? She learned early on she had more melanin in her than the other kids in the neighborhood. Everyone was always quick to point out she looked "darker" than her brother and sister. She even had some aunties and uncles who would joke that her mom had "jumped the fence" because she did not look like her white dad or siblings. As big brothers often do, her brother once joked that she was adopted. She believed it for a time. She hated white dolls.

As the little girl grew up, she realized she was allowed to cry and carry around a doll that peed and made awful noises, but she was not allowed to do things boys were allowed to do. Her family went to a church where she was expected to wear a dress. She was expected to wear itchy, uncomfortable tights. She was expected to wear shoes that were slippery on the ice outside in the winter and pinched her toes. Boys could wear pants and comfortable shoes. She hated wearing dresses because she couldn't run, jump and sit the way she wanted to. She realized that was why they made girls wear dresses. She began to be controlled in ways she didn't like.

The church had meetings where once you are older, the girls are separated from the boys. The boys were taught to do things. They were told they would be future leaders of the church. Only boys could serve sacrament and hold leadership roles. She would notice only men would sit on the elevated chairs at the front of the church. Girls were expected to be nothing more than good little followers.

The little girl would sometimes go to the women's meeting with her mom. The meetings always focused on "homemaking" and talked about ways women could be better moms and housewives. Little girls were taught to be passive women when they grew up. Being "reverent" was a word her church leaders used a lot. She felt the same way about the church her family went to as she did about her dolls. Useless and boring. Being expected to dress and behave differently from the boys at church made her want to rebel. She thought the idea of sitting and being "reverent" just because she was a girl was bullshit.

The only place the little girl felt wild and free was on the playground at school during recess. It was the only place she was not expected to behave like a girl. She could even dress like a boy at school! She wore jeans, sneakers, and a football jersey. Even though her mom told her to, she didn't wear underwear because there is no point in it. Her hair was long, dark, wild, and full of tangles. She never fixed it and rarely combed it. She hated to have her hair neatly fixed in pretty braids and ponytails with lovely barrettes like the other girls. It hurts to have your hair pulled and fixed in ways that please others. Boys didn't fix their hair, so she decided she didn't need to either.

When she was on the playground, she could run until her lungs burned, climb everything in sight, scream as loud as she wanted and throw things as hard as she could just like the boys. She could hang upside down and swing on the monkey bars until her head hurt. She said "fuck" and "shit" because for some reason it felt liberating to express herself in an "irreverent" way, especially on Monday mornings after church the previous day. If a little boy bullied her, she kicked his ass. No one fucked with her. It was on the playground she felt free, like a boy.

Eventually the little girl grew up. She started to wear makeup. She liked dressing like a girl because when she dressed like a girl, she felt sexy because she had a tight, curvy ass and perky boobs now. She got zits. She got her period. She could not understand why some girls were so excited to get their period. She hated it. She realized the division of boys and girls and the roles they play was finally complete. Teenage hormones were suddenly the secret sauce that solidified the divide between how boys and girls are allowed to act in society.

Although the hormone monsters were quickly taking over

her teenage brain, the girl tried to stay friends with her male friends for as long as she could. The boys were fun. She got bored just sitting and talking about boys with girls. When she would hang out with her male friends, they would always do stupid shit together. She loved skipping school with the boys, chugging cheap beer, passing around a skunk weed joint, cursing like a sailor, and shooting shit up in the nearby hills. She was allowed to act like a fucking wild woman when she hung out with the boys, and she loved it.

She had crushes on girls and crushes on boys and couldn't understand why it was so shameful to like girls too. Her first real tongue kiss was with a girl. She had a secret girlfriend who she made out with all the time. Eventually they stayed friends but dated boys because they were not allowed to let anyone know they liked each other. She and her girlfriend were a shameful, dirty little secret. The church said it was a sin. She knew by the way people talked about "faggots" if anyone found out she liked a girl rather than a boy they probably would call her that too. The punishment and ostracization of dating another girl would have been too much to bear, so she shoved that part of her so deep down inside of her soul she forgot it was there.

When she was in high school, she was horny, but she learned fast it was not ok for girls to be horny like boys. The boys at school were cool if they were horny. Horny boys were "studs." They were open about their sexuality while the girls suppressed their desire to have sex because it would make them "loose" or a "skank." Boys were even more cool if they got to finger a girl and brag to their buddies "smell my finger" in the locker room. Girls were theirs to sexually experiment with. Touching tits and going even further made a boy "cool" while it made a girl a "slut." The more a boy had sex, the cooler he was.

If some boys didn't have sex, they lied about "getting pussy" to be cool. High school boys bragged about their sexual exploits totally uncaring about how hurtful and shameful it was for a girl to be called a "slut." The girls called you a slut too. The other girls also made fun of girls for being fat. The worst thing ever was to be fat and a whore. Boys were never labeled fat whores. In fact, the girls could be far more venomous to one another and treat other girls far worse than any boy could. She quickly learned it gave her a false sense of power to join the queen bee bitches who ran the social hierarchy of her high school and call other girls sluts too. Aside from being afraid she would also be bullied by them, she never understood why she wanted the approval of the queen bee bitches.

In the girl's high school, you could even be branded a slut even if you never met the guy who lied and said he fucked you. The girl had a lot of guys claim they fucked her. Most didn't. They lied. She was damned if she did and damned if she didn't fuck someone. Some queen bitches even said, "she will be pregnant before she even graduates from high school." The girl was branded a slut and whore by the second month of her freshman year in high school.

The girl quickly learned her innate sexual desires were something to be ashamed of. She learned that if she had sex with a boy, her body was used at a catalyst to make him a man while she was socially stamped as an easy little whore. She didn't understand why boys thought girls' bodies were something to dominate then ridicule as a "piece of ass." If anything, she felt she was the one who fucked the boys she had sex with, not the other way around.

She also learned that masturbation was a sin in her church. She was taught to save herself for marriage, but the girl had no desire to date nor marry one man for the rest of her life. She quickly learned the best way to survive high school was to suppress her true self. She learned to put her inner wild in a deep dark hiding place where she did not feel tempted by her. Her inner wild became something she needed to expel, to get rid of. Her inner wild was nothing but trouble. Releasing her inner wild could cause her to live a life of banishment, bullying and shame.

Society and her religion won. The girl conformed. She obeyed. She followed the pack like a good little girl. She became reverent and even a little bit popular. She stopped messing around with girls and boys and denied her sexual desire. She never really fit into one clique but joined the queen bee bitches and talked shit about other girls to fit in. She learned to giggle like a little girl when a popular boy said nearly anything, even though he was far from funny. But she giggled because it was expected of her, and it made the boy feel even more manly and in charge. She learned how to boost a boy's ego above her own. She learned that when she performed what was expected of her for others, society embraced her and when she misbehaved, she was shunned.

The girl became a woman. At work she learned to never interrupt a man in a meeting because he would just keep talking over her anyways. When men talked at work everyone listened. When she would talk, she was often interrupted by men, and everyone would instantly turn their attention to whatever the man was saying. When she was able to share even a few sentences she spoke quickly to say as much as she could before she was interrupted. She was often "mansplained" at work. It was very difficult for her to provide input and get her ideas across to the team at work, so she just stayed quiet. She learned her voice didn't matter as much as the men's voices.

Once she was mansplained so hard her coworkers complained about their misogynist boss's behavior, and he issued an email apology to the team. Little did they know he had texted her and asked her out just a few months before. He was married. He was an overgrown frat boy who used women as chattel to boost his fragile male ego. He was also lazy. He barely showed up to work and made the highest salary there. She didn't say anything about his sexual harassment because he controlled the HR department. She would be fired in an instant. As a white, entitled male he had all of the power and he enjoyed taking advantage of it. She had none so she kept her mouth shut and cried in the bathroom stall at work.

One time at work there was a gag gift exchange. A male coworker gave her a brunette Barbie doll in a bikini. She fantasized about punching him in the fucking face, slitting his tires, even poisoning him. The rage inside of her was at a full boil. While she stared at the Barbie doll the man who gave it to her giggled like a child until his face turned red. He thought he was hilarious and so did everyone else. It was clear she could either be pretty or smart, not both. She put on a brave face but as soon as she could she went into the bathroom stall at work and sobbed. She cried in the bathroom at work a lot. She felt as worthless as the plastic bobble head she had stuck to her dashboard in her car. From that day on, she wore glasses and smart suit jackets to look less like a Barbie. She even deepened her soft voice in meetings to better be heard. She realized work was just one big fucking high school.

    Eventually the woman became a leader at work. Her first "big job" was to take over a leadership position formerly occupied by a man. She later found out although she had far more education than her predecessor it turned out she was offered $30,000 less a year than what that lazy piece of shit earned. She cleaned up the pathetic mess the man left behind. She learned her worth and bravely negotiated her salaries moving forward. She made damn sure her voice was heard, or she would leave an organization. The woman did what she was supposed to do. She looked good on paper and had a fancy career title. She worked hard enough to be able to only choose roles where she could work with male and female leaders who respected women in the workplace and promoted diversity.

    Even as an adult, the woman felt ashamed of her inner wild, so she became an expert at suppressing it. No matter how empty inside denying her true nature made her feel, she put on a great performance as society cheered her on for her good behavior. Even though she knew her inner wild was her true nature, she rejected it as much as society did. The call of her inner wild constantly reminded her something was missing. As she tamed her inner wild to make others happy, she felt her own joy slipping away. Her inner wild was an undeniable part of her burning desire to live life on her own terms, but she knew women who behave the way they are expected to get through this thing called life with less heartache and shame. The woman did what she was supposed to do, but she thought it was bullshit.

The Art of Re-Wilding

"Maybe Eve was never meant to be our warning. Maybe she was meant

to be our model. Own your wanting. Eat the apple. Let it burn." - Glennon Doyle

Does the little girl's story have a happy ending? Damn right it does. How do I know? Because that little girl is me. Please allow me to introduce myself. My name is Aimee, and I am here to fuck shit up – but in a beautiful way. I am here to teach you how to re-wild. My greatest hope and wish in writing this book is to help you embark on a journey of self-discovery to get in touch with your true self by reconnecting with your inner wild to feel greater joy in your life.

I would like to explain why I use the word "womxn" rather than "women" in the title of this book. Traditionally and linguistically the word "woman" has included the word "man". In addition, the term "female" has used the word "male". The term women is used to intentionally include all humans who identify as a women, including transgender women.

This is not a book about the battle of the sexes. If anything, re-wilding can help you experience more loving, stronger relationships with the opposite gender. I wrote The Re-Wilding of Womxn to help women (with an "x" and all nonbinary humans) reconnect with their true inner "wild" selves to experience and manifest self-love and brave well-being & live their best life on their own terms.

Re-wilding can help you experience better mental, spiritual, and physical wellbeing. Re-wilding helps you feel good, and when you feel good more good things happen. When you re-wild the law of attraction begins to apply to you. You become a great attractor of all things good in the universe.

Your Inner Wild

You may be wondering what exactly is involved in the process of re-wilding. Let's begin by exploring what re-wilding means. Re-wilding is defined in scientific and human ways. Most often we hear about rewilding in environmentalism defined as a way of reverting a piece of land back to its original state. Original state refers to the wild and natural state of the land before humans came in and messed it up by overtaking the land's natural processes and over domesticating it. When environments are depleted by manmade damage their growth slows or stops altogether. The environment begins to die and become a wasteland. Re-wilding is also referred to as the process of reversing domestication. Antonyms offered as the opposite of re-wilding range from subjugated, tamed, trained, mastered, broken-in, subdued to domesticated.

This scientific definition also metaphorically applies to the re-wilding of women. Put plainly, the re-wilding of women can be defined as a return to our natural state of being before we were domesticated and trained by societal forces. As our natural and wild state is removed from us, we begin to lose our joy. Our ability to grow and thrive is diminished. Our intuition becomes muted. The human power of domestication of women takes the form of societal approval when women behave according to gender roles strictly assigned to females. On the flipside, when a female acts in a way that goes against societal roles for women, she is punished, shamed, and ostracized.

Re-wilding is interwoven into the fabric of all female humans. Understanding the art of re-wilding begins by allowing the little girl inside of you to finally grow up the way she was meant to. It is allowing yourself permission to reconnect with your inner wild child before she was shamed away into hiding when she didn't act the way she was trained to. Re-wilding is a process of unlearning the many ways society has taught you to feel about yourself. Re-wilding is a rebellion against the many ways society dictates everything about how you should look, love, and exist.

Re-wilding is a return to yourself. It is an undoing. Re-wilding is an awakening of your body image, sexuality, female roles and learning to love yourself regardless of others' approval. Re-wilding is facing our biggest fears and doing the things girls aren't supposed to do. Whether you take small or big steps towards your re-wilding, how you choose to re-wild is up to you. Every woman's re-wilding journey is deeply personal and unique.

Aimee Callahan

Forever Wild

In spite of the many domesticating moments, you may have experienced as a young girl growing into a woman, your inner wild is still very much alive inside of you. You were born wild and no matter how out of touch you may be with your inner wild she still is an integral part of who you are. She is the true you. "Within every woman there is a wild and natural creature, a powerful force, filled with good instincts, passionate creativity and ageless knowing." Dr. Estes nailed it when she describes women as a powerful force. Your inner wild is your powerful force unique only unto you. My daughter has grown up riding horses, so I have spent a lot of time as a horse mom at the stables. I have often witnessed horses being trained and "broken." I see the horses whinny, resist, buck and run during the process. The wilder horses are the harder to domesticate, just like us. Each time I see their wild spirit tamed a part of me feels sadness to see their wild disappear. I can picture them running free with their pack in the wild far away from humans.

In their natural habitat, wild horses live on their own terms. They feed off of the land and sleep under the stars. The hardest part for me to see is once a wild horse is tamed, they lose their wild forever. They often spend their lives living in a horse stall. Rather than grazing freely in a pasture, their meals are served to them by us.

But just like us, not all horses can be domesticated. I met a horse, appropriately named Challenger, who refused to be tamed. Depending on his mood, he allows riders from time to time, but Challenger refuses to live in a stall. He kicked the stall door incessantly until they finally let him out to pasture. Because he refused to be tamed, Challenger gets to spend every day grazing and roaming free in a large open meadow.

When I see a horse tamed, I am reminded of how we, as women, are expected to be domesticated as well. We are expected to behave in certain ways that may subjugate our true natures and often during the process there is a chance we lose the ability to tune into what makes us special. Every one of us has a special inner wild that we can tune into to experience greater happiness, positive change and success in life. Your inner wild is what sets you apart from everyone else. It is your unique gift.

Nothing About You Needs to Change

I didn't write this book to try and change you. That is the last thing you need to be told to do in your life. As women we have already changed enough about ourselves to make others happy. We have bended, flexed, contorted, and distorted every part of our mind, body and soul to make others happy. We learned from an early age to take care of everyone else first and put ourselves last. Women don't need to change. We need to celebrate ourselves exactly as we are.

I wrote this book to remind you there is absolutely nothing about you that needs to change. Nothing. Reread this as many times as you need to for it to resonate deeply within your heart, mind and soul: Nothing about you needs to change. All that you need from life is already inside of you.

As women we are surrounded by messages all day in society, social and mass media and even in our conversations that serve as pressure cooker reminders about how we "should " live our lives. These messages are inescapable, and it can be challenging not to drink the Kool Aid and allow ourselves to be trained how to live and act as women, especially when we receive approval and acceptance for behaving in ways that kill us inside to make others happy. Re-wilding allows you to live the life of your dreams, free from the judgment of others. It is ok to live life on your own terms and not live your life the way society tells you to. You were born wild and your inner wild, the true you, is your greatest gift.

I am here to remind you "well behaved women rarely make history" and your inner wild can help you experience greater inner peace on the inside and success on the outside. Your inner wild has a rightful place in the world, and she deserves to be set free. Our goal is to on a journey together of rediscovery of your inner wild.

All you seek in life already exists inside of you. As women need a nurturing reminder of how powerful we truly are when we connect with the most beautiful parts of ourselves. Half of my life I have experienced the domesticating influences of society due to my gender, and the other half of my life I have spent tearing down the invisible prison bars built around me based upon how society thinks I should live my life because I'm a woman. When I chose to embrace my inner wild, I experienced greater happiness and success in my life, work and relationships. I invite you to do the same. You deserve to live your very best life!

We are going to take a deep dive into what it takes to re-wild, to fully embrace your true self each day of your life. I look forward to accompanying you on your personal re-wilding journey so you can better celebrate your beautiful inner spirit in positive ways that bring you joy and wellbeing in all areas of your life. It is also my sincerest desire that after you finish reading this book you will confront your inner mean girl and confidently ask her if she needs a fucking hug.

Let's re-wild.

Chapter 2: Find Your Inner Wild Child

"Within every woman there is a wild and natural creature, a powerful force, filled with good instincts, passionate creativity, and ageless knowing. Her name is Wild Woman." -Clarissa Pinkola Estés

Dying to be Reborn

*Author's note: This chapter contains graphic violence. Please read with caution or skip this chapter if you are concerned about triggering past trauma you may have experienced.

I survived an attempted murder, and it was my inner wild that saved my life. I am sharing this story with you for two reasons. First, I want to reassure you that you are much stronger than you may even know. Never underestimate how strong you are when you need to be. Second, your inner wild is brave. She is fierce and she will fight to the death to keep you safe. Your intuition is the voice of your inner wild. You can trust your inner wild, she is here to guide you.

The night, or actually the early morning, I almost died went something like this.

Somewhere in my sleepy haze I woke up to an earth-shattering boom and the cracking sounds of wood breaking. This was the sound the man in black made to break into my shabby little rental house.

Boom! Crack! Boom! Suddenly beginning to realize this was not a nightmare because I was awake, I froze. The man in black standing over me was death staring me in the face with a terrifying look of unshaking determination. The moment had arrived. It was time for me to fight or die.

My adrenaline rushed so intensely I felt like I could not breathe. I felt like I was having a heart attack. I was a broke, single mom sharing a bed with my two-year old baby. I immediately felt an intense need to protect her too.

Adrenaline has stuck with us since we were cave people running from saber tooth tigers and when you feel sheer terror it can flood your body and mind so intensely it is a total shock to your system. In my terrified state I reached for my cell phone and without effort he took it from my hand and placed it in his jacket pocket. He then grabbed me by one arm and with little effort on his part, pulled me out of my bed and into the living room. As he dragged me toward the living room, I grasped at anything I could. As I tore my nails off one by one desperately grasping at the wall it did nothing to help. He dragged me into the living room with little effort.

My mind was spinning. Utter terror took over me as I immediately realized how helpless I was. I was like a flimsy little ragdoll in his hands. He was much larger and stronger than me. He threw me around in a way that let me know he was in total control of me. Once in the living room he forced me on the couch and told me "I'm not leaving here until you're DEAD." "I'm going to slit your throat from ear to ear".

His eyes were pure rage. They were fully dilated pitch black. I have never seen anyone's eyes look like this before. He was not human. He was not of this world. He was a force much darker than anything human.

Filled with a feeling terror I cannot even begin to describe, I realized at that moment this is how my life would end. I was facing a horrible, violent death. Until this moment I was a little deer in the headlights. I don't know how to fight! How could I possibly fight off this strong man? I didn't have a choice. As my adrenaline slowed a bit it became like a magic serum feeding thoughts of survival to my brain. My adrenaline transformed my mind into a clear-thinking survivor. I tried to talk to him--he was not having it at all. In full survival mode, during this moment of intense fear I remembered a book I had read by Gavin de Becker called "The Gift of Fear." He told the story of a woman who was about to be killed by a man in her home. She survived because she bravely refused to be a victim and silently followed him down the hallway of her apartment and slipped out alive.

It was like a clear message from my guardian angel. The woman I read about was brave. She was a survivor. She fought to live. I knew I needed to be brave too. I knew my only chance to live was to fight harder than I had ever fought before in my life. My life depended on it.

My little girl helped save my life. She was two years old at the time and was sleeping with me in bed that night. She is a heavy sleeper and slept through all the mayhem up to that point. At that moment my daughter came walking out into the hallway looking for me asking "Mommy?" My heart sank. I would do anything to protect her. I didn't want her to see me die, especially in such a horrible way. I begged him "please put her in the bedroom so she won't have to watch?" It was like a switch went off and something in his eyes and demeanor and he suddenly seemed human. I felt an indescribable sense of relief when I saw him agree to put her back into the bedroom. She would hear what would happen, but at least she would not see it.

As he was putting her in the bedroom, I saw my escape. As I was no longer pinned to the couch, I jumped over the couch ottoman and ran into the kitchen where I had a large can of bear spray on the top of the refrigerator. Living in Wyoming, I always took bear spray hiking with me. He was on me immediately. I turned around and sprayed him directly in his eyes less than 2 inches away. I kept my finger pressed on the bear spray trigger and thought to myself "I don't care if I get sprayed too. I will fumigate this cockroach".

While fighting for my life I was screaming at the top of my lungs to try and get my neighbors to hear. He immediately tackled me to the kitchen floor where I banged my heels on the floor as loudly as I could to try and wake up the neighbors downstairs. I had experienced too many stalking events with this individual and when I moved into that particular house, I made sure there was a family in the basement who could hear if something ever went wrong. That preliminary decision saved my life.

Aimee Callahan

The moment I feared the most and my intuition kept telling me was inevitable was happening. I knew this man would come after me one day. I knew he would try to kill me. I knew if he didn't get what he wanted, I was supposed to die. That night I fought harder than I knew I could. I fought to breathe. I fought to live.

As he was trying to kill me, I refused to give up. He was incredibly strong, but I was not as weak as he thought. I refused to allow him to murder me and my right to be a mother from my beautiful child. He had no right to try and snuff out my light and steal my life. Our fight eventually moved to the living room. My face, eyes and skin were covered in bear spray.

The next thing I knew he wrestled the bear spray from me and suddenly he had me in a reverse choke hold and my feet were hanging above the floor. I was going to die from him choking me to death. He had won. I lost my ability to breathe and knew at that moment this is how my life would end. My legs kicked furiously and as I lost oxygen my feet were kicking then just began to flutter. I could feel my life being choked out of me moment by moment. This man was willing to stop at nothing, to go to prison or worse, just to see me dead. This realization was gut wrenching. The man who to had broken into our home to murder me was my daughter's father.

As I desperately struggled to keep breathing, I knew I couldn't last much longer. I was going to die.

As life was being choked out of my body, I felt unbelievable anguish over losing my life in such a violent, horrible manner. As I fought to take my final breaths, I began to accept the horrible fact this is how my life would end. What happened to the girl who was so independent and used to believe she could do anything? What happened to the girl who backpacked foreign countries solo? As I struggled to stay alive, I felt an indescribable sense of deep sadness that I would not be able to raise my daughter. My right to be her mother was violently being taken away. Even to this day, as hard as I try to find the words, I simply cannot begin to describe the sense of deep, dark despair I felt while dying.

Then, a miracle happened. A police officer burst in and yelled at my attacker to let me go. My attacker refused and tightened his grip on my neck. The police officer tackled him to the ground within seconds. I just remember hearing furniture and the TV flying through the living room and suddenly I was free. I ran as fast as I could to the front door. When I reached the door, my eyes finally swelled shut from my bear spray. As my eyes were closing, I saw a man in a blue uniform and his bright metal police badge glowing in the porch light. I think I hugged him. I cannot remember. He rushed in to help stop my attacker. It was literally a blur at that point. All I know is I felt an immense sense of relief I never knew was possible.

I made it outside safely. I was in pure shock and standing on my front porch in my underwear screaming at the top of my lungs covered in bear spray with my eyes swollen shut. This was an out of body experience for me. I could hear someone screaming from a distance and I knew it was me, but I could not connect with being able to stop screaming in terror at that moment. I was somewhere else entirely.

What I remember next is hearing the police take my attacker out of the house past me to the police car. The police also got my daughter and wrapped her in a blanket and gave her a teddy bear. They put me in the front seat of their warm police car and put her in my arms. I just sobbed. I cried harder than I have ever cried in my life or probably ever will. We had gone through absolute hell, but we were ALIVE. And as for that adventurous, independent girl I once knew who backpacked solo overseas? Well, she was still here.

Later the officers told me when they opened the door to get her, she was standing in the bedroom staring straight ahead with her mouth open and her whole little body was shaking. I still have that teddy bear the police gave my daughter that night. I still don't know why, but I also saved the tiny pajamas she was wearing that night. Maybe I saved them because it made what happened seem less surreal. Perhaps I saved them to remind me that my little girl helped save my life.

Before I spent the next few hours at the police station the officers grabbed my glasses from the house so I could see when my eyes began to recover from the pepper spray. Having all been pepper sprayed themselves, they offered advice on how to best remove it. When my eyes began to open, I remember one of the officers washing my glasses for me. The police officers were extremely compassionate and kind. They are my heroes.

Dying to Be Reborn

That night is not how my story ends. In many ways it is how it began. In previous domestic abuse situations when he would attack me, I shut down like a deer in the headlights. I didn't know how to fight back. I always froze in fear and shock at what was happening. That night I didn't shut down. I trusted my inner wild when she told me I needed to fight or die trying.

The next day, I remember feeling extreme joy erupting from the trauma I was also suffering. I survived an attempted murder! I had won because I chose to fight for my life. I won because I walked away with my life and my daughter had a mom to raise her. I was so grateful as I realized I was very close to being six feet underground.

I was laugh-crying the entire day. My body was in pain. I had fought so mightily that I could not even turn my head to the side for almost a week because it hurt too much to do so. Every muscle in my body ached from fighting so hard. My inner wild saved my life. I chose to look fear in the face and fucking fight to the death. I never knew I had that strength inside of myself. The power of my inner wild surprised me. It was then that I realized one truth I do believe we all share, and that is to never underestimate your will to survive. Never underestimate the power of your inner wild!

My life went on. I am grateful for being alive every day. I am beyond blessed to be alive to raise my daughter. No matter how awful I may feel at some moments I am grateful to be alive to feel the pain. Acute stress and PTSD are no joke. When my therapist told me I had "acute stress" I jokingly told her "There is nothing cute about it!" At least I still had my offbeat sense of humor. For weeks after the attack, I heard the echo of my screaming in my mind. I would be in the middle of teaching my class at the local community college and I could hear my screams in my head loud and clear like some type of haunting background noise.

Alongside the acute stress and PTSD kicking in was a new shadow of myself. My shadow follows me everywhere I go. I still panic at loud noises, especially if a sudden noise is loud enough to wake me up. My friends and family know not to jump out and scare me as a joke as it literally spins me out into a dizzying panic attack. I don't watch movies where women are running for their lives. It brings back too many bad memories for me. Believe me, I have put in a lot of work to heal and even still I have a long way to go. But this new shadow of myself is strong as nails. She won't go down without a fight. In fact, she will fight to the death.

Divine Intervention

The universe had my back that night. From the time my neighbors heard the front door break in, to the time the police arrived, the entire event lasted only three minutes. It was only three minutes. Three minutes. When I found out how much my life could change in three minutes, I knew I needed to appreciate each moment I had to breathe freely, raise my daughter, walk my dachshund, to stop and admire the bees on brightly colored flowers and to basically carpe diem, Latin for "seize the day," every damn day.

After a few years, the police officer who saved my life told me a story of divine intervention. He was ending his night shift and getting ready to get off of work. The timing worked out to where when my neighbors called 911, there was a shift change going on. He overheard the call come in. Rather than call it quits for the night he told me he ran to his police car and drove as fast as he could to my address. If he had arrived even seconds later, I may not be here. The universe works in mysterious ways. That night she worked to bring me the man who would save my life. I am grateful he chose to fight too.

I received many gifts from my near-death experience, mostly that I gained an unstoppable zest for being 6 feet above ground and a feeling of being absolutely unstoppable because by the grace of my higher power and the universe and all of their powerful forces working together I am alive. I regained a strong relationship with my higher power. I embraced the universe for saving me that night and every day since.

I will never doubt the universe has my back ever again. Along with your inner wild, the universe will never fail you. They are best friends and work well together. We will get into a deeper discussion on that in a later chapter.

From Victim to Warrior

My attacker served just under five years in prison. To this day he claims he doesn't remember doing what he did, but he was wisely lucid enough that night to speak only these words to the police, "I want my attorney." I learned so much from almost dying. I also learned to forgive someone who was not sorry for trying to kill me. I am proud I chose to fight for my life that night. I was brave. I AM my inner wild.

I was a victim. I fought to become a survivor. I forgave and became a peaceful warrior. It took years but I finally managed to let go of my anger. I forgave his actions that night for my own freedom to experience joy in my life. My forgiveness does not erase the past, but it allows me to reflect upon it with compassion for what I survived. Most of all, my forgiveness set me free from the anger and immense hurt that was eating me up inside for years. Trauma can shut your heart down. But I refuse to stop loving. I learned to love myself harder than before.

The events of that night gave me a higher purpose in life. There is a saying, "Don't waste your pain, use it to help others." I was given the gift of life for the second time. My survival experience became a higher calling for me. Helping others helps me heal. I have chosen to dedicate my life to helping women re-wild and live their best lives on their own terms. If my story can help even one person, then my goal of sharing my story is complete.

Now that you know your inner wild will help in traumatic events, it is important to know your inner wild can also help you feel a daily dose of happiness. As busy adults, we are all familiar with the stress of everyday life. As women, we are often balancing multiple roles as mothers, wives, partners, daughters, and more all while balancing busy careers. We experience how difficult it is to feel joy in stressful moments. However, with enough practice you can learn how to quickly transform stress into joy. In the next chapter you will learn how to use your inner wild to have more fun! It is impossible to feel stress when you are having fun. Through discovering and practicing your now and zen, you can begin to experience a greater sense of overall happiness and well-being.

Chapter 3: Awakening Your Inner Wild

"All good things are wild and free." Henry David Thoreau

The Art of Now and Zen Motorcycle Riding

Buying a Harley-Davidson motorcycle changed my life in unimaginable, amazing ways. My motorcycle instantly made my life more fun. Prior to buying this two-wheeled speed demon, I was immersed in being a full-time parent, finishing graduate school and ferociously building my career so I could afford daycare and put food on the table. After experiencing the threat of being homeless far too many times as a starving student and single mom, I was willing to do whatever it took to make sure we had a roof over our heads. I was consumed with school, work and parenting. My personal priorities took a backseat as I was intensely focused on making ends meet. Does this sound at all familiar? Giving all we can during our children's early years are part of what we often do as women and moms.

As a single mom, I did not have much of a personal life until my daughter was in elementary school. During her daycare and preschool years, I collapsed into bed exhausted every night. Any free time I may have had during the day I happily chose to take a nap and watch Spongebob Squarepants with my daughter rather than go on a date. I couldn't get enough of her. I truly soaked up every adorable moment with her as a teeny, little human.

When I did venture out on a dating app to meet a stranger, 99% of the time they did not even remotely look like their photos. I experienced so many cases of false advertising during my online dating years I rarely, if ever, dated. It was slim pickings out there and I did not meet anyone who was worth shaving my legs and giving up naps for. So, rather than waste what precious free time I had to myself on app dating potential serial killers, I chose to spend every spare moment I had with my daughter. When my daughter turned six, I bought my first motorcycle. She has grown up riding on the back of my motorcycle. We have a blast when we ride together!

The Best Thing You Can Do with Your Clothes On

I always say riding a motorcycle is the best thing you can do with your clothes on. For my first moto, I did not buy just any motorcycle, I bought a 2013 Harley-Davidson '72, a remake of the 1972 Harley-Davidson chopper-style motorcycle. She had bright gold candy flake paint, chrome spoke rims and whitewall tires. When you buy a motorcycle, it is a tradition to name your bike. She was a spicy 1970's wet dream on two wheels and so her name was destined to be Disco.

When I bought her, I had a stage one race tuner added, which is another way of saying I made her a hell of a lot faster than she was when we met on the factory floor. Disco was loud, snorty, loved to speed and was completely obnoxious. She regularly set off car alarms. She was untamed and that is exactly how I felt when I was riding her. I can straight up tell you there is simply no way to describe how it feels to put a powerful V-twin engine in between your legs that hits triple digits above the speed limit within a quarter of a mile. When I rode her, I was transformed from a highly responsible, overworked women into an outlaw circa Mad Max. I feel like Annie Oakley must have felt in her wildest moments. There are simply not enough words in the dictionary to describe the freedom I feel when I straddle my bike and put my knees in the breeze. Fun doesn't even begin to describe how I feel when I ride my motorcycle.

Finding Your Now and Zen

Your mission in this chapter, should you accept it, is to have more fun! The process of re-wilding is fun. Re-wilding makes you feel great inside and out. One way to instantly connect with having fun is to discover and connect with your now and zen. Your now and zen is an activity, hobby or side gig that electrifies you. Your now and zen is an expression of your inner wild. It makes you feel alive inside and joyfully grounds you in the present moment. When you are in your now and zen the last thing you are thinking about is work or paying bills. Your now and zen is something you love doing.

When we engage in our now and zen, we often set our inner wild child free. That little girl inside of you that used to run wild and free as a child is allowed to come out and play. Keep in mind, your now and zen is not a mindless activity that allows you to "zone out" so scrolling through social media and binging Netflix do not count! Your now and zen comes from your soul and centers you in the present moment.

Being in the present moment is healthy for you. When you do something you love, you are not dwelling in the past nor worrying about the future. When you engage in an activity you are passionate about, you gracefully exist in the present moment. The more we can embrace being in the present moment, we feel an increased sense of peace and wellbeing. The saying "stress can kill you" is real, and we often feel the most stress when we worry about something that hasn't even happened yet. Technically, worry does not exist because we are focusing on a mythical event that may or may not occur. Be that as it may, we often worry as adults so a great way to release stress in life and feel instant joy is to let loose and have more fun!

There is a quote by Kelsey Grammar describing what it feels like to celebrate your now and zen, "Prayer is when you talk to God. Meditation is when you're listening. Playing the piano allows you to do both at the same time." Whether you enjoy hiking, cooking, music, horses, gardening, art, crafts, dancing, skydiving, or playing sports, our now and zen provides an instant reprieve from the daily stress of adulting so you can let loose and have fun. At the end of this chapter, we will do a now and zen discovery activity because you deserve to have as much fun as you possibly can.

From Zero to Instant Zen

One of the fastest ways for me to reach my now and zen happy place is to ride my motorcycle. I'm free to be at one with my inner wild. I am alone yet connected with others riding with me. When I am flying down the road on two wheels I am at peace and zen. Riding is like meditating, it requires my mind to focus on the present moment. The moment I hear the rumble of my engine start, riding grounds me in a way that allows me to listen and talk to my higher power at the same time. Riding can be as risky as it is exhilarating. I feel like I am dancing a beautiful, sexy tango with life.

Riding also combines my passions. I am passionate about being outside in nature and traveling to new places. I have an insatiable gypsy soul. Riding allows me to feel an abundance of amazing sensations at one time. All five of my senses are fully engaged. At the same time, I am focused on safety, I am soaking in the joy of the ride. I admire the beautiful blue sky. I smell fields of dewy wildflowers. I love the smell of gasoline and oil on the road baking in the sun. I ride into beautiful sunsets. I traverse twisty mountain canyons with frothy rivers roaring alongside me.

I have been caught in sudden rain storms I didn't see coming on the doppler radar and hidden under bridges like a troll waiting for the rain to pass. I have gotten lost in beautiful places I never knew existed. I have ridden to places like the top of Beartooth Highway in Montana and truly believed that if there is a heaven that is what it must look like. I have ridden along the Pacific Coast Highway and marveled at the sparkle of the ocean glistening in the sun beside me. The map of places and possibilities of new riding adventures is endless.

Riding connects me to the power of Mother nature. I have major respect for her because she is the boss. Mother nature makes the rules and determines how my day on the bike will go. I am constantly checking the weather, wind speed and clouds in the sky to make sure I am prepared for whatever the road may bring. I am always on the lookout for potholes in the road, gravel and oil spots that can make my tires slip.

When I ride, I'm often on roads surrounded by wildlife. Dusk and dawn are happy hour for elk, deer, antelope, coyotes, and most wildlife who can wander across the road in front of you in a moment's notice. I even came close to hitting a dead deer in the middle of the road that suddenly appeared when I rounded a sharp curve outside of Steamboat, Colorado. I once had a moose cross the road right in front of my bike on the way to Yellowstone National Park outside of Dubois, Wyoming. I have glided by snakes, mountain sheep, tarantulas, armadillos, and snakes. I have also ridden by bison in Custer National Park in the Black Hills in South Dakota.

Riding reminds me of the saying by Eckhart Tolle, "Realize deeply that the present moment is all you ever have." Because I am laser focused on my safety and surroundings I am always in the present moment on my motorcycle. I am not dwelling on the past nor worried about the future. I am fully in sync with my inner wild when I ride my motorcycle.

Awakening Your Inner Wild

I love the quote, "Stay young and wild as long as you can." I suppose the opposite of this quote would be to feel "old and boring" which clearly none of us deserve nor want. Take a moment to think about how many hours you work per week. And yes, being a stay-at-home mom counts as work and then some. As a stay-at-home mom you don't get to clock in and out. You are on the clock 24/7, 365. Now compare the hours you work to how many hours you have fun per week. It is likely the ratio is not remotely comparable. It is a fact of adult life that we work far more than we have fun.

There is a reason so many of us are dying far too young from stress-induced diseases. Adulting is stressful and it's difficult to have fun when we are busy working. We spend far too much time as weekend warriors detoxing from the previous work week. By the time we feel refreshed it is Monday morning and time to clock in again. It is important to take time to awaken your inner wild child and enjoy your life as often as possible. As adults we may not have as much free time as when we were kids, but we can carve out now and zen moments that count.

As I take you through a stroll down memory lanes of my childhood growing up as a wild child in a small town in Wyoming, take a moment to ask yourself if there is anything you miss doing from your childhood or even in recent years. If so, I encourage you to go out and do it!

I suppose I was always destined to ride a Harley. I grew up as one of the kids in the "my parents sent me to play outside until the streetlights came on" generation. Like most of my peers, my childhood years were spent playing outside without the distraction of the technology we have today. I grew up in a small town in southwest Wyoming called Green River. It was too small of a town to be dangerous. Everyone knew each other from work or church. It was common for our parents to basically kick us out of the house to go play outside.

My small Wyoming hometown sits near the Flaming Gorge reservoir, and we spent summer days at "the Gorge" camping, hiking, dirt biking, swimming, and water skiing. Most everyone had a boat and once each icy cold winter ended, we were always out enjoying the water. My dad regularly took us kids fishing and hunting. We would often be out in nature regardless of the weather. I remember him coming home many nights with icicles hanging off his red beard from being out in the mountains all day.

I had a unique father. My dad always said he was born "200 years too late." He was a modern-day mountain man. He was once a logger in Alaska, and we even went to the forest each year to cut down our own firewood. I have memories of being deep in the forest and out of town "as far from people as possible," just how my dad preferred it. Wyoming was an amazing place to grow up. For me, Wyoming will always be my true home state. It was also a great place for me to leave when I graduated from high school. I was too wild to stay there. My gypsy soul needed to live out in the world.

My dad lived for adventure, and I inherited his wild nature. During my childhood, we would spend most winter weekends on the ski slopes nearby in Utah. He was an expert skier and taught me to ski in his tracks. My dad was a Marine. He always pushed me to do my best, sometimes a bit too hard. I remember the second time we went skiing he took me up to an advanced slope. I was crying and too terrified to follow him down the mountain. He said, "Get your ass down this mountain right now." So, somehow, I did. All I know is that within just a few years, I was following him down the slopes no problem and then breaking off on my own to do backcountry skiing with my equally adventurous friends. We were wild and free in the fresh powder.

When I was in junior high, my dad gave me a 4-wheeler ATV. During the summers I would ride it all over the nearby hills and down by the river. I felt free and rode far faster than I should have. The other kids with dirt bike motorcycles and ATVs would meet and we would spend the day vrooming around in the dirt kicking up dust. Once we even found a mud field and rode in the mud all day. I came home covered head to toe in mud and my mom refused to let me in the house until I hosed off outside first. During those days we would laugh without abandon until our sides hurt. We did not have an adulting care in the world.

It is important to connect with your inner wild child because your inner child knows how to have fun. As women we need to create our own opportunities for fun or we will literally be all work, parenting and no play. Please remember to take time in your life to celebrate your now and zen. We only have one life as we know it, we must be sure to nurture our minds, bodies and souls with as much fun as possible! Let your inner child run wild and your adult self will thank you.

Your Vibe Attracts Your Tribe

Only two months after I bought my motorcycle, I wrecked. I was wearing my helmet, boots, and leather gloves but it was 99 degrees outside and at the last minute I put my leather jacket in my saddlebag. That was a mistake. The scar on my left arm now serves as a permanent reminder to wear my leather jacket when

I ride. The wreck left me with some road rash and was pretty bruised up. I remember pulling asphalt pebbles out of my left arm. I was terrified to ride again, but I rode my motorcycle to the repair shop the next day. My knees were shaking the entire time, but I was glad I dusted myself off and faced my fear of riding by getting "back in the saddle" again.

When I decided to buy a motorcycle, I had no idea I would end up joining one of the most supportive, empowering sisterhoods in the world. One of the most amazing gifts we receive from re-wilding is we open our energy up to meet others like us. After my motorcycle accident, I decided to put my bike up for sale. I was new to Denver and didn't have a lot of friends. I was hoping the bike would be a fun hobby and I looked forward to riding through all of Denver's nearby Rocky Mountain canyons. I listed the bike for a great price. I was even willing to take a loss. To my surprise I didn't even get a nibble of interest in the bike. It was as if the universe was refusing to let me sell the bike.

Though I had decided to sell my motorcycle, I still had a tugging feeling I didn't want to give up the motorcycle without first experiencing the joy of riding. When I saw there was an all-women's event in Denver, I decided to overcome my fear of riding and go. I was so nervous when I started the bike. I remember as I rode south on the freeway to the event my odometer clicked over to 1,000 miles. I had not realized I had ridden that many miles as a newbie.

When I rolled into the event, there were already hundreds of bikes parked and women gathered together. I limped the bike in and after awkwardly parking the bike, once I shut off the engine I was approached by a woman, named Jaclyn, who simply said, "Nice bike." It turns out she was also from Wyoming. We rode together the rest of the day and met other women. That event was over nine years ago. She and I are still close friends.

Frida Kahlo once said, "She was not fragile like a flower. She was fragile like a bomb" and that is the best way to describe the women I know who ride motorcycles. If you have not yet experienced women who are at one with their inner wild, much less hundreds of them gathered at one time, I encourage you to attend a women's only motorcycle event. My tribe of fellow women who ride quickly expanded and we are thousands strong and are connected in a positive way on social media across the globe.

Female riders are currently the fastest growing demographic of people to buy motorcycles. The riding sisterhood is local, statewide, national, and international. We are a global sisterhood. When I ride with these women, I cannot emphasize how riding forms a bond among us that is simply indescribable. We are instantly bonded by our mutual love of riding and the freedom it offers us. We respect each other's space on the road. We trust each other with our lives.

Riding motorcycles is a great equalizer. My riding tribe consists of women who are stay-at-home moms, pilots, lawyers, entrepreneurs, truck drivers and the list goes on and on. We come from all different backgrounds, and we are all ages, shapes, sizes, and skin tones. The global sisterhood of women on motorcycles welcomes all women, period. Our conversations rarely touch upon work as we tend to lean towards talking about our motorcycles. We also love to share riding stories with one another. We love to empower each other. The women who make up my riding tribe are loving, fierce, alpha, and unapologetic. They have had a tremendous influence on my ability to love myself. I appreciate the sense of unconditional love they show me. Since these bad ass women love me, I have no excuse not to love myself!

I swear this to be true. Your vibe attracts your tribe. I constantly say this to my daughter, best friends, colleagues and basically anyone who will listen. We are what we put out to the universe. If you experience a loss of connection with certain individuals once you connect with your inner wild, please be reassured there are fellow women like you in the universe. Once you create the space to welcome your own inner wild, be prepared for the universe to introduce you to others who also celebrate their inner wild in similar ways. Your inner wild will never leave you alone. There are others like you, I promise.

The Freedom is Worth the Risk

When people find out I ride a motorcycle they often respond one of two ways. The first typical response is "that is so cool!" The second response is along the lines of "I know someone who died in a motorcycle accident." I am truly sorry for your loss, but you don't need to remind me I can die riding my motorcycle. I know riding a motorcycle is dangerous. We motorcycle riders also tend to be superstitious because we know we are living a risky lifestyle. We understand we can die riding a motorcycle and most of us consider being reminded of that as bad luck. We have all been to funerals of dear friends we have lost in the wind. We know every summer we will lose even more friends. We know people who have died in motorcycle accidents too.

Many riders lose their lives due to drivers who are texting while driving. We riders refer to people in cars as "cagers" because we really do see being stuck in a car as being locked in a cage. I have been cut off far too many times in traffic by people staring at their phones. These drivers never even realize they could have killed me.

I do the best I can to stay as safe as possible. I ride defensively. I stay out of your blind spot. I am always watching you. If you are on your cell phone I stay as far away from you as possible. I would like to continue raising my daughter into an adult. If you are too close to my tail end, I will let you pass me. To those of you who drive while texting I can only say this, "PUT YOUR FUCKING PHONE DOWN."

So why risk your life riding a motorcycle, especially when cagers who text are a constant death threat? To this I can only respond that I would rather die a good death than live my life in fear. I would rather be dead than oppress my inner wild.

If given the choice, I would rather die riding my motorcycle than in a cubicle at work. My personal philosophy on how I would prefer to die was solidified a few years ago when I learned of a coworker who had a heart attack and died in her cubicle at work. It was heartbreaking. I made my work husband and assistant extraordinaire of five years, Bill, pinky promise me that if I were to start to die at work, he would at least drag me out to the sidewalk to die as far away from my office as possible or I would come back and haunt him every day.

I have occasionally been berated for being a single mom

and riding a motorcycle. These judgmental bystanders can kiss my wind chapped ass. As soon as I bought my bike I did my will, living will and power of attorney. I put my affairs in order just in case. All motorcycle riders have their own unique views on death. Most will tell you "If it is my time then it is my time." This is because those who think motorcycles will kill you usually don't ride. I also share the view that I can get hit and killed by a bus just as easily as I can die on the motorcycle. I do not think that just because I bought a motorcycle, I will die riding it. When it is my time, it is my time. I won't waste the precious life I have living in fear. And if riding a motorcycle decreases my chances of dying in a cubicle at work, then so be it.

So, why do I ride? It's simple. The freedom is worth the risk and my inner wild deserves to be free.

Your Now and Zen

Now that I have shared how I connect with my inner wild, you may be wondering about yours. The very fact you are reading this book means you are meant to be here! You now know your now and zen is an expression of your inner wild. Your now and zen comes from your soul and centers you in the present moment.

In this chapter I asked you to reflect upon how much you work compared to how much you have fun. You were asked to reflect upon childhood or recent memories of doing something that makes you feel happy. I now invite you to do a quick five-minute self-reflection and journaling exercise that can help you discover and connect with your personal now and zen. I encourage you to start a re-wilding journal in a notebook or on your computer. Have fun exploring your now and zen!

Journal Exercise: Your Now and Zen

Let's take a moment to explore your now and zen. For the next five minutes, I encourage you to brainstorm and write down an activity (or activities) you are passionate about that connect you to your now and zen.

Keep in mind, your now and zen is not a mindless activity that allows you to "zone out" so remember social media and Netflix binging do not count! Your now and zen comes from your soul and centers you in the present moment. Often our now and zen may be an expression of your inner wild.

After you explore your now and zen activity (or activities) that connect you to your inner wild, your true self, take a moment to write about how you feel when you engage in your now and zen. What is it about your now and zen that makes you feel most alive? Do you allow yourself time for your now and zen? If not, how can you create space to practice your now and zen more often?

I urge you to keep your journal nearby and refer to it as many times as you need to to help you stay centered and focused on releasing your inner wild.

Now that you have explored your now and zen, you are ready for the next step in your re-wilding journey. You are now ready to face the big bad wolf, also known as your greatest fears. Sometimes, re-wilding can feel scary. You may suddenly find yourself face-to-face with some of your deepest fears. When it comes to fear, you will learn to "name it to tame it" and recognize when fear may be holding you back from living your best life. You will learn how to distinguish between fear versus your female intuition, the voice of your inner wild, which is here to guide you safely through life.

Chapter 4: Taming the Big Bad Wolf

"She slept with wolves without fear, for the wolves knew there was a lion among them." R.M. Drake

A few years ago, I booked a solo trip at a yoga retreat in Costa Rica. While booking my yoga retreat in Costa Rica I had a panic attack. This was one of my bucket list items for years, but fear almost stopped me from going. I asked my friends to join me, but no one could go during that time frame, so I decided to go alone. Not having friends to travel with never stopped me from getting my passport stamped before. I didn't understand why I was so scared. I often travel alone. I even backpacked through most of China by myself. I could not understand what I was afraid of. Was it my intuition telling me not to go or was I afraid for no reason?

We often confuse fear with our intuition. We know re-wilding is fun. We know it makes us happier. We know it can deepen our relationships and connections with others. We know re-wilding even benefits our mental, spiritual, and physical health by removing needless stress from our lives. If we know re-wilding is good for us, why do we hold ourselves back from embracing our inner wild? The answer is fear. You are now ready to learn how to recognize your fear versus intuition to help you re-wild in a positive way that makes you feel good.

Gypsy Soul

I am a gypsy soul. I have an insatiable lust for travel. I love to travel with friends and by myself. Before I became a parent, I lived in China and taught English at a university there. While in China, I backpacked solo through most of the country and visited nearly every major city including Macau and nearby Hong Kong. It was an exhilarating adventure. My stay in a Buddhist monastery in the mountains was a life-changing experience. I visited villages where no foreigner had ever been before. I stayed in hostels where I met other foreign travelers like myself also traveling on their own. One of the best things about traveling alone allows us space to meet so many exciting fellow travelers on the same frequency as you. If I had been traveling with friends, I may never have met these fellow adventurers and heard their stories.

  I am also addicted to adventure. One of my favorite adventures backpacking through China was climbing Mount Tai, revered as China's most sacred mountain. Confucius climbed Mount Tai to feel closer to heaven and write poetry. Chinese emperors climbed Mount Tai to honor the sacredness of heaven and earth. With over 6,000 hand carved stone steps the holy mountain peaks at around 5,069 feet tall. Being raised in the Rocky Mountains, a mountain that is less than a mile high does not seem too rigorous a climb but is far from a leisurely mile hike. It may not be a Colorado 14er, but Mount Tai is a steep, rigorous climb.

  A friend of mine had climbed the mountain a few weeks before and made the mistake of wearing his heavy backpack while going up the mountain. I felt excited nervousness when my friend, who was in peak physical condition, told me he could not make it to the top and two of the locals had helped him reach the summit. I had left my backpack at the hostel at the base of the mountain and was determined to see the sunrise from the top of the mountain. I set out early that morning and began my climb. I was immediately met by the most amazing scenery and quickly made it to the top of the mountain in time to see the sunrise. In my excitement to get to the top I had not thought about the trek down. There is a cable car option from the top of the mountain halfway down Mount Tai, but I wanted to fully enjoy the climbing experience, so I descended the entire way step by grueling step. I quickly felt my legs turn to mush on my walk down. My muscles literally felt detached from my leg bones. Thankfully the locals there sold walking sticks for $1 to help you get down the mountain. I bought a cane and limped down the mountain much slower than my climb to the top. Once at the bottom of the mountain my legs were in so much pain I went back to the hotel and rented a room with a bathtub and soaked my legs in hot water before my evening train to Beijing. After weeks of traveling and staying in hostels with shared bathrooms, a private bathroom with a bathtub and running hot water was an absolute luxury I was lucky to take advantage of.

The Breakthrough

After my years of traveling through China and other places, I could not understand why I was so afraid to go to Costa Rica alone. It was not like I was in my twenties staying at international backpacker hostels. I was a grown up with a career now and had booked a high-end luxury retreat and spa and had airport to resort transportation arranged. The resort planned everything for visitors like me from the moment I got off the airplane to the moment I boarded my flight home. Despite my history of solo travel, I had actually not been out of the country since I had my daughter. My Spanish was choppy at best, and I was nervous to get my passport stamped after so many years. I quickly realized I was feeling fear because I had grown safe and comfortable, even complacent, in my daily routine. Which is ironic because getting away from my daily routine and taking a much-needed break was exactly what I needed.

I faced my fear of traveling alone and went to Costa Rica and I had a life-altering breakthrough moment there that would change my future decisions in life and work. While I was there, I rode a horse on the beach. I swam in the ocean. I hiked through the jungle and soaked in pools under waterfalls. I stayed in a gorgeous resort and woke up to meditate on a gorgeous wooden deck overlooking the ocean. I fell in love with the sounds of the jungle. The overlapping howls of the howler monkeys permeated the silence of each peaceful morning. I did yoga at the end of each day while the geckos chirped their evening songs. I ate amazing farm to table food and exotic fruit all day every day. I saw howler monkeys, geckos, parrots, toucans, lizards and had a friendly coatimundi follow me around the resort for half a day. I fell in love with the healthy pace of life in Costa Rica and living "la pura vida," the pure life.

I had gone to Costa Rica with no expectations of having any life-changing moments. My goal was simply to get on the plane and go and relax in a new place. This was also during the not-so-distant time in my past I was not yet self-aware of the fact I used work to self-medicate my PTSD. I was suffering from major career burnout from pushing myself too hard. I was burning the candle at both ends and had worn myself out. To say I was running on fumes is an understatement. I would soon discover I was using work to numb my pain.

We ended a yoga session one morning lying in Savasana when I had a surprise spiritual experience. Savasana, pronounced "Savasana" in Sanskrit (the language of yoga), is also referred to as corpse pose as it is an excellent reminder of our own mortality. Savasana requires you to lie on your back with your eyes closed, and arms and legs relaxed with your palms facing up. The reason savasana is sometimes referred to as the most challenging pose in yoga is because the art of letting go can be challenging. If you want to take it a step further, you can use your time in savasana to practice letting go of all ego and attachment to cravings and desperation we feel toward worldly desires we mistakenly think will make us happy. In savasana, there is nothing to do but just let yourself "be" in the present moment.

While meditating in savasana our yoga teacher guided us to visualize ourselves at the end of our lives. What would we think about? Who were we at the moment of our impending death? I was hit with a massive realization that if I am in a situation where I do have time to contemplate my life before exiting this world my career would not cross my mind. My daughter would fill my mind. I would look back upon the times in my life I felt love. I opened my eyes and suddenly felt completely overwhelmed. I cried with immense gratitude and relief.

Ever since the attempted murder I had used work as an escape from deep emotion in my life and I had not even realized it until that moment. This hit me like a ton of bricks but in a liberating way. My trauma was following me around like a dark shadow

I was fighting off every day. I knew I could no longer work at the pace I was. It was not sustainable. Something had to give and continuing to overwork myself was no longer an option. I needed to get a life. PTSD steals your emotion from you. I needed to feel again.

Fear Can Set You Free

My experience in savasana that morning in Costa Rica set me free. Although it would take a few more years to achieve it, from that moment forward I realized I deserved to have a better work-life balance. I left the yoga retreat with my body and mind completely invigorated. My soul had been recycled.

I am so grateful I faced my fear of traveling alone again. Rather than allow fear to cancel my trip, I explored, unpacked, and pushed through my fear. I was rewarded with a beautiful reminder to focus on life more than work. Work is not therapy. After looking inside of myself, I recognized my fear. I forgave myself for what was a natural fear response to facing an unknown place and situation and I had not yet traveled to another country alone after becoming a single mom.

There is a saying I love and appreciate that resonates deeply for me, "You say you are willing to die for your children but are you willing to live for them?" I realized at that point I was not living my life to the fullest. I had grown complacent, and I was wearing myself out by not allowing myself a break for far too many years. My fear of leaving my daughter and going to a foreign country momentarily paralyzed me. I am so glad I overcame my fear of traveling alone, remembered who I was before my career changed me, and went to the Costa Rica yoga retreat because it was an incredible physical and spiritual experience.

Imagine if I had canceled my trip due to fear? I learned something amazing. I was braver than my fear and I deserved to live my best life. So do you. I came back from my Costa Rica trip a little bit better than I was before. I am grateful for overcoming my fear and the transformational experience I had. It can be scary to face what we want most in life, but the reward is worth working our way through our fear. You are more powerful than your fear.

When you work through fear to connect with your inner wild, fear cannot hold you back from living your best life on your own terms.

The Culture of Fear

As a culture, we live in a society guided by fear. My graduate school thesis for my master's degree in Communication and Journalism focused on the use of fear by mass media as a tactic to keep us glued to the television. I did a study on ways mass media manipulates our perception of our world. I won best thesis that year. Media and social media keeps our attention by bribing us with fear. Our media seems to live by the mantra "if it bleeds, it leads" leaving us feeling we live in a society where we need to feel fear constantly. A good friend of mine calls the news "spiritual poison." Social and mass keep us hooked by feeding us fear every day, and we all too often innocently buy into it.

It is difficult to accurately perceive reality when we are constantly inundated daily with social and mass media messages telling us we should be afraid. Research shows the more we engage in watching the news and crime shows on television the more we think the world is a dangerous place, even when crime statistics may be low. Our perception of fear can skew our overall sense of safety. Do you ever notice how your local news will also throw in a feel-good story about a puppy to barely offset their constant stream of negativity? The powers that be working in the media industry know that only the negative will lose your attention over time, so they insert feel good stories about puppies as a tactic to keep you hooked.

Dr. Wayne Dyer reminds us, "The law of attraction is this: You don't attract what you want. You attract what you are." One of the most important things we can learn is to fully understand why we are born to feel fear and how it can fool us or help us. Our fear is meant to guide and inform us, not throw us off balance. Fear can be a very powerful emotion. Rather than let fear dictate your feelings and decisions, you can learn to tune into fear and hear the messages fear sends to help you. When we are misaligned with fear, we literally block the good we deserve in life. The result is we often make irrational fear-based decisions preventing us from living our best lives. One way to effectively navigate fear is to learn to recognize what type of fear you are feeling. It is important to identify if you are feeling impending GTFO Fear (fear with a capital "F") or fear of the unknown (with a little "f") which we feel nearly every day.

The GTFO Fear

GTFO Fear or get-the-fuck-out fear with a capital "F," is an unmistakable fear that clearly warns you when you are in danger. The night I was almost murdered I felt GTFO fear. You know the feeling when you come close to getting into a fender bender, suddenly your body is supercharged with energy, you feel short of breath and your mind feels spun out? GTFO fear activates our sympathetic nervous system fight-or-flight response causing your body to be flooded with stress hormones (adrenaline) so you can react quickly to survive. GTFO fear is the kind of fear you also feel when you have a phobia. Phobias are an odd anomaly. One person's phobia of flying may be another person's spider phobia.

I recently had an experience that I can describe as legitimate GTFO fear. I have felt the intense thrill of riding my motorcycle just a few feet past bison gathered on the side of the road in Yellowstone National Park in Wyoming and Custer National Park in South Dakota. I was surprised to discover you can also have the same experience of riding through herds of bison less than 30 minutes from Denver at the Rocky Mountain Arsenal National Wildlife Refuge. The Rocky Mountain Arsenal National Wildlife Refuge is a 15,000-acre area of land dedicated to protecting deer, coyotes, bison and many other native species of plants and wildlife.

Let me just start by saying it is incredibly thrilling to see bison without a safety fence. I always enjoy it but appreciate keeping the recommended viewing distance of 25 yards. Bison are the heaviest land animal in North America, with bulls (males) weighing up to 2,000 pounds and cows (females) weighing up to 1,200 pounds. Having grown up in Wyoming I have a deep respect for their space and my not leaving in an ambulance. I even have a gorgeous bison tattoo on my left forearm.

Every year we hear of tourists in Yellowstone who get absolutely obliterated by a bison for getting too close. I have had a friend who got rammed by a bison while on her motorcycle in Custer National Park in South Dakota and she has had multiple surgeries and complications walking ever since. She also stopped riding her motorcycle. Sometimes on the motorcycle you must ride by them, which is ok. Riding through bison, chances are you may not be ok. I love the thrill of adventure, but despite the risks I take I try to put myself in as few situations as possible where I can get seriously injured. I don't like pain and I have a high health insurance deductible.

The road ahead was full of bison. A few bison were lying down in the road. There was also a cluster of bison standing in the middle of the road. A female with her calf thundered by us where we stood on the side of the road. You can feel the powerful force of their weight make the ground shake when they run by. I thought of my friend who was charged by a bison and remembered all of the ambulances I see screaming to the rescue inside Custer National Park at Sturgis each year, all due to someone getting too close to a bison.

My adrenaline started to rush, and not in a good adventure kind of way. We were the only people on motorcycles there. My friend wanted to ride through them. I explained to her that although they look cute and fluffy, they are not big puppies, and they are known for seriously injuring and even killing people who invade their space. Cars backed up on the road to view the bison and we kept our distance and pulled over to wait and see if the bison would eventually move from the road. They didn't move.

Cars passed them by on the shoulder of the road, but we cannot easily ride our street motorcycles in the weeds and dirt, especially with my friend being a new rider. At this point, the refuge becomes a one-way road. It is a wide road so there was plenty of room to turn around and go back the other way. Turning around would keep us safe. We did not have to walk and wind our bikes through the bison lying in the road. We would have been surrounded on all sides and they would have been less than three feet from our bikes and the sound of loud motorcycles scares them. I decided I did not want to make that phone call to my best friend's mom in

Brooklyn that she was mauled by a bison in Denver and advised we turn around and go back the way we came.

As we turned our bikes around to go the wrong way down the one-way road there was a man in a minivan who started yelling at me for going the wrong way. As he was yelling at me his husband in the passenger seat rolled his eyes and looked at me like "Oh no, here we go again." I got the sense the driver could often be a grumpy bear (no pun intended). He would rather have had us rammed by a 2,000-pound animal than go down a wide road the wrong way down a one way. I kindly informed him I would not risk our lives riding through a herd of bison just because he wanted us to follow the one-way rule. I also invited him to ride bitch on the back of my bike if I did. He yelled a hearty "Fuck you!" I continued to lead us out of the refuge going the wrong way down the one-way road.

Fear is clear with us when it tells us to stay safe. When your fear tells you to get the fuck out of a place or situation, listen to it regardless of social pressure. When it comes to GTFO fear, don't let what someone else wants you to do interfere with your safety and wellbeing. In spite of the social pressure to put our safety in severe risk I chose to "break the rules" and get us home safely. We got home safely and in one piece. The angry man and my friend from Brooklyn got to view the beautiful bison lounging in the sun and making the ground thunder as they ran around with each other in their natural habitat. It was a beautiful day.

Fear of the Unknown

GTFO fear screams at us while fear of the unknown nags at us. Fear of the unknown, or everyday fear with a small "f", is hardwired in our amygdala, the lizard part of our brains. Our fear-based lizard part of our brain promotes safety, not higher intelligence. Our fear-producing lizard brain is purely reactionary, not thoughtful. It causes us to be overwhelmed with debilitating emotion. It is important to recognize our fear-based lizard brain for what it is. It is not the brightest bulb. It serves one purpose only, to keep you safe.

Fear has helped us survive as a human race since we lived in caves. It is a part of our natural survival instincts. Fear can be our greatest friend and protector in certain circumstances. Fear is also our natural, biological go-to response, especially when we feel deep emotion. Believe it or not, fear exists to protect us. Beautiful things exist on the other side of fear.

You are now prepared to unpack your fear of the unknown so irrational fear does not hold you back from the benefits of re-wilding. Our everyday fear of the unknown is the kind of fear that interferes with our ability to make positive life changes. To embrace our gift of fear, we are going to examine the daily dose of debilitating fear we often feel that can leave us feeling afraid of pursuing our dreams and life goals.

Fear feels scary because it requires facing the unknown. Fear of the unknown explains why it can be so frightening to sleep without a night light or swim in a dark lake. Since we don't know what is in the dark, and as cave people we stayed out of the dark to survive, fear is doing its job by always trying to keep us safe. Fear can do too good a job of trying to keep us safe. Fear can be a healthy messenger or an irrational emotion that can cause us to make decisions with negative consequences. However, when we face our fear for what it is, we can often reap the rewards of overcoming being held back from fear. Sometimes with fear the monster is the messenger. What also lies on the other side of facing our fears can be beautiful.

We all have a caseload of irrational fears. Take a moment and ask yourself what you are afraid of losing the most. Many of us are afraid of losing our jobs. We are often afraid of losing the love of someone we care about. We often have the unthinkable fear of losing a loved one. We are often afraid of being hurt or rejected. I hope it is reassuring to know that all of these fears are completely normal and rational as they are a part of your innate gift of fear.

Have you ever felt joy from watching your child or pet sleeping then in the next moment have a terrifying worry something awful is going to happen to them? This is our natural fear triggering us to protect our loved one. I always felt this fear kick in while watching my daughter sleep as a baby. I still have this fear kick in when I watch her leave to go hang out with her friends. Fear always reminds me my daughter is literally my heart traveling outside of my body.

When it comes to daily life, emotions of fear of facing the unknown can be easily misinterpreted and leave us feeling worried and off balance. It is also irrational fear that turns into needless worry. Although we have evolved from living in caves, our brains have not. When it comes to fear, don't believe everything you think. Our perception defines our reality and if it is guided by irrational fear, it may be faulty.

Don't be afraid to examine fear sensations as they arise. It can be uncomfortable, but I promise it is worth it to take a moment to recognize your fear as irrational or legitimate. Sitting with your fear can also help you better identify what you are feeling and help you recenter and focus on the present moment. When fear sneaks up on you, ask yourself, "Why am I feeling fear?" — "What am I afraid of?"

I encourage you to journal about your fears to explore them more deeply. Listen to your highest voice within you to examine your fear before you make decisions in your life based upon your fear emotion. Trust your intuition to help you unpack your feelings of fear in a way that makes sense to you and leaves you feeling safe, loved, and moving forward in a positive direction.

Fear v. Intuition

Now that you have learned how fear can be the big bad wolf to scare you away from manifesting your best life, you are ready to explore the many ways your intuition is your spiritual tour guide past fear. Your intuition is the voice of your inner wild. When we talk about intuition, we are talking about those gut feelings we get that often inform our most important life decisions. Our gut feelings often start in our body and are powerful thoughts that demand to be heard. When something just doesn't feel right, even though we may not be able to logically explain it at the time, our gut feeling is telling us a clear message.

Some believe our gut feelings are guardian angels or our ancestors watching over us. Have you ever ignored a gut feeling only to find out later there was something wrong about that person or situation your gut warned you about? Gut feelings are the voice of your intuition. Intuition is our deeper sense of knowing that without a doubt protects us and guides us towards a life filled with greater purpose, joy, and self-love. In short, intuition is seeing with your soul.

We are going to explore how you can connect with your intuition. To understand how fear and intuition manifest themselves in your life it's important to learn how they react differently in your mind and body. For starters, intuition and fear are generated from different parts of our brain. Scientists believe intuition is generated in the right hemisphere of our brain, the area of our brain responsible for imagination and creativity.

You now know fear arises from your amygdala, the almond-sized lizard brain area of the temporal lobe of your brain responsible for emotional responses. Therefore, intuition feels like knowledge and although we do feel it in our body, it does not carry much emotion whereas fear causes us to feel intense emotion often accompanied by a racing heart and a rush of adrenaline. Fear can cause you to feel mentally and physically constricted (adrenaline rush, shortness of breath, mind spinning, etc.) while your intuition has the power to positively expand your awareness.

One major difference between fear and intuition is when we feel intuition, we are neither stuck in the past or future. Your Intuition talks to you in the present moment. Intuition is zen. Fear is focused on the past or future, which is why fear often transforms into needless worry.

More specifically, our fear is often generated from past psychological wounds and is focused on something that "might" happen. Intuition whispers to us while fear often yells at us. Intuition occurs naturally without conscious reasoning. Also, your intuition is never wrong. Your intuition is a neutral form of knowledge guiding you toward positive change whereas fear can often hold you back in life. Fear puts out the guiding light of your intuition. Intuition provides an encouraging, gentle nudge in a positive direction whereas fear can often dictate our thoughts and actions.

Fear is an external trigger that can arise out of trivial circumstances ranging from a change in your job description to our reaction when watching the news. Most importantly, our intuition shows up to help us tune into our inner wisdom when we are facing life's major decisions.

Women's Intuition

Women make incredible spies. It turns out that as women, we are hardwired to have powerful intuition. For decades intelligence agencies, such as the CIA, preferred women as spies due to the fact we have heightened intuition that allows us to intricately read social cues, body language and people skills. We have an extra antenna when it comes to our intuition. The saying "women's intuition" is real and there is a scientific reason why we do not call it "men's intuition."

Male and female brains are wired differently. This does not make one gender better or worse than the other, it just means our brains are different. It is important to mention, there is ongoing debate about the gendered brain. My goal is to offer information on what our key brain differences are that lead to our heightened intuition. Some scientists believe our brains have key differences due to evolution, and research studies also show our brain development is also influenced by socio-cultural factors. Women have strong intuition that has evolved over centuries of raising children while also preparing food and other life duties. As women we have evolved to quickly switch tasks, when necessary, which often requires us to effectively access both sides of the brain.

The corpus callosum, the region of the brain that connects the right and left hemispheres, is thicker relative to overall brain size in women than men. Women also have more neural connections which allows us to better tune into our social and emotional surroundings. It is believed a thicker corpus callosum allows women faster access to both the right and left-brain hemispheres, which leaves us prime candidates for intuitive decision making. According to Dr. Judith Orloff, MD, Assistant Clinical Professor of Psychiatry at UCLA and author of Guide To Intuitive Health and

The Empath's Survival Guide, "Women are also psychologically more in touch with their emotions (perhaps because they've been given more cultural permission to be this way) and are more likely to integrate hunches, emotional 'hits' about people and logic." Contrary to our innate biological fear response we have passed down for generations, we don't know where our intuition comes from, but we all have it. We just need to listen to it and fine tune it over time.

Thank you, Intuition!

You have likely heard the saying, "female intuition does not lie." How many times have we had experiences and we look back and think to ourselves, "I had a gut feeling that was happening." Intuition is a strong messenger, whereas fear is a biological response. Another wonderful advantage of your intuition is that it can help you navigate your fear. When your intuition is speaking to you it is important to trust what it is saying.

I was years into a relationship in my 20's to a man who was so physically beautiful it was extremely difficult to keep women away from him. He was incredibly fun, outgoing, and charismatic. I was not the jealous type, but he worked in a networking business so needless to say he was surrounded by female admirers nearly every night. He loved the attention he got from women. What guy wouldn't? I didn't think much of it and accepted interacting with admiring women was a part of his job. One night I suddenly woke up from a deep sleep very late one night about two hours after he said he would be home. He recently started coming home at all hours of the night and early morning using the excuse he had to stay late at work.

That night I had an overwhelming feeling to get in my car and drive to his job. I was instantly awakened and full of energy by this overwhelming sensation and curious to see if I was incapable of trust in a relationship or if my intuition was right. In the past, when I had begun to ask questions about why he was keeping odd hours I was dismissed as being "crazy." Sound familiar? I cannot tell you how many other women have told me similar stories. My intuition was so clear that night it felt like a voice talking to me that would not stop unless I woke up and drove to his work. I drove to his workplace. My intuition was right. When I pulled up to see him with another woman in the middle of the night, I thanked my intuition for helping me see what the rest of my life could have been like had I stayed in that relationship. Thank you, Intuition!

It is ok to allow, welcome and even celebrate your intuition. I try not to have regrets in life, but I can say the times I have regretted the most in my life have been due to my completely ignoring my intuition. I have wasted a lot of time and cried far more tears than necessary due to the times I chose not to listen to my intuition. Part of the process of re-wilding is trusting your intuition. You likely have a similar story. It just takes a bit of practice to learn how to easily recognize when our intuition is guiding us. No matter how hard we try and ignore our intuition, it is always going to be there to guide us through life. We only need practice on how to discern between whether we are experiencing intuition or fear.

Name it to Tame It

You can tame your fear before it has a chance to tame you. Practicing the ability to distinguish the difference between fear and intuition can not only keep us safe but can help us experience a greater sense of joy, positive change and wellbeing in life. When you lean into your intuition you are better able to open yourself up to the amazing possibilities life has to offer. Your intuition is part of your inner wild. She is there to protect and guide you. You can also use your intuition to tame your fear so it does not hold you back.

When you are able to recognize your fears, you can learn to "name it to tame it", giving you the ability to approach fear with self-compassion. Read and repeat the following affirmation until it feels like second nature:

"My intuition is here to guide me safely through my fear to help me live the life of my dreams."

Now that you have learned more about fear versus intuition, let's practice recognizing the feelings that intuition and fear can produce in your mind and body so in the future you can trust your intuition to help you move forward in a positive way.

Self-Reflection: Name It to Tame It

In this exercise you will explore the differences between fear and intuition. You will explore ways to better tune into and listen to your intuition and conquer your fear to live your best life on your own terms. Allow yourself time to write and reflect on the following questions. I encourage you to write out your responses in your re-wilding journal.

Allow yourself time to dig deep and reflect on the following questions. I encourage you to write out your responses in your re-wilding journal.

Exploring Your Fear

What is a fear you have that may be holding you back in life? It could be losing your job, moving to a new state, traveling overseas, starting your own business or something that gets you nervous. What do you fear the most? How does reflecting on your fear make you feel? What is the worst that can happen if you conquer your fear? How would facing your fear help you live your best life on your own terms?

Now name your fear. Write down your fear. For example, my recent fear that was holding me back was "traveling alone." Please take a moment to to actively explore your fear by filling in the blank below and repeating the affirmation as many times as you need to:

I am braver than my fears. I can choose to _____ and live my best life on my own terms.

Intuition: Take a moment and imagine someone or something (a child, pet, partner, family member, etc.) and focus on the feeling you have when you think of them. You are likely feeling a highly focused feeling that resonates in your mind and body. That is similar to what intuition feels like. Remember your intuition is the voice of your inner wild. Now reflect on a moment when you know your intuition was sending you a clear guiding message. Take a moment to sit with this sensation. Memorize it. Name it. Welcome it.

Conclusion: Take a moment to summarize ways intuition and fear feel differently for you. Now that you know how to distinguish between fear and intuition, how can you better tune into your intuition moving forward?

Congratulations on exploring your fear versus your intuition. Facing your fears is challenging work, but the rewards of working your way past your fear lead you to the beauty that exists on the other side. Always remember you are braver than your fear and you can trust your intuition, the voice of your inner wild. In the next chapter, you will learn ways to use self-love as a superpower. Self-love is another re-wilding tool you can use to help you experience greater mental, spiritual, and physical wellbeing.

Chapter 5: Your Inner Wild is Your Superpower

"There are two emotions: love and fear. Everything that's love can't be fear, and everything that's fear can't be love. You're either in one or the other." **Dr. Wayne Dyer**

At the risk of sounding cliche, as I am sure you have heard this before, true love starts with you loving yourself first. Your inner wild thrives when you love yourself! Self-love is not selfish, it is essential for our mental, spiritual, and physical health. When you love yourself, you can enjoy life on a full emotional gas tank. Your inner wild is your superpower. Re-wilding is the key to untangling and freeing ourselves from years of being trained as women to behave by suppressing our inner wild. Our energy is contagious to those we love, and it is hard to pour from our cup when it is empty. Like the airplane oxygen mask analogy, it is critical you allow yourself to breathe freely before you can save your children, which is also why self-love can be so hard for us as women.

One of the ways our inner wild is domesticated is by being trained as young girls to put everyone first and ourselves last. A critical component of re-wilding is to practice self-love. Taking care of ourselves first flies directly against all we are taught as women. It is instilled in us at an early age that self-sacrifice equals love. Often, we feel guilty if we put ourselves ahead of our family members and those we care about. We also grow up watching other women model behavior prioritizing others ahead of themselves. We see our mothers and grandmothers take care of our families.

We see them as strong matriarchs to the extent they are often the glue that holds families together. Aside from these women being our moms and grandmas, what do we really know about them? We often define women by their capacity to nurture others. As a result, as women we are taught to feel shame when we take time for ourselves and practice self-love.

Neglecting yourself leads to burnout. We crash and burn when we constantly put others ahead of ourselves without taking care of ourselves first. We are better at helping others when we nurture ourselves. In this chapter, you will learn to move past the societal guilt assigned to all women if they don't put others ahead of themselves. This chapter is all about self-love. We are going to unpack the ways we hold ourselves back from our inner wild. We are going to explore a journey of re-wilding and ways you can re-connect with your inner true self to live your greatest life on your terms. We are going to dig even deeper inside what makes you truly shine your brightest. You will learn ways to start prioritizing yourself in positive ways even when facing adversity. At the end of this chapter, we will practice self-love affirmations and you will have an opportunity to reflect on ways you can realistically add more self-love in your life. Let's begin by exploring ways you can ditch your inner mean girl.

Ditching Your Inner Mean Girl

"We don't see things as they are. We see things as we are." **Anais Nin**

I recently had a conversation with someone who knows me better than anyone. I told them about my desire to make a huge career change and start my own consulting business. I had put myself last for years. I was overworked and I was running on fumes. I needed a career change or the stress I was under was going to make me crash and burn. When I told her about my dream to make a serious career shift she said:

"You are too young in your field, no one will take you seriously."

"You have only worked in higher education, you don't have any business experience."

"You are just an average girl from Wyoming. What makes you special enough to have great minds hire you?"

"You have a high voice and no one may take you seriously."

"Maybe you should just 'suck it up, buttercup, and revisit this when you are closer to retirement so you are taken more seriously."

I did not feel very confident about forming my own consulting business after this conversation. You may be wondering why I would be friends with someone who would be so critical of me, especially when I went to them for support. Who needs enemies with friends like this, right? Well, this "friend" was ME. This was my own inner mean girl self-talk. I was holding myself back before even getting started. I was my own worst enemy.

If I let my inner mean girl take over, I would never pursue my dreams. I pushed past her negativity and decided to give it a shot. I had nothing to lose. I was going to hit a wall soon and I needed my work to move in another direction. I rejected my inner mean girl. I trusted my inner wild and let the universe do the rest. I ventured out on my own and within less than three months my consulting was off and running. Soon I was consulting full-time and working on exciting projects that revived my soul. My passion for my career returned.

Self-love isn't just a corny new age fad. We live in a constantly changing world where good enough is rarely enough. Often, we are held to very high standards, especially as women, and as a result we tend to be way too hard on ourselves. When we are pushing ourselves beyond to achieve external recognition our inner mean girl kicks in, and she is the opposite of nurturing. Oscar Wilde said, "to love oneself is the beginning of a lifelong romance." Self-love also attracts the love you want to receive back in life.

Loving ourselves is much easier said than done. Being female, we have not been given permission to love ourselves first, so we need to give it to ourselves. Like the need to eat and drink for our physical survival, we need to practice self-love every day, all day for our mental, spiritual and emotional wellbeing. When you care for yourself, you are able to better connect with your inner wild to experience greater inner peace and happiness. And here is another benefit, your positive energy is contagious to others.

Nothing helps you to ditch your inner mean girl faster than self-love! Practicing self-love creates an environment for your life light to shine brightly not just for yourself, but for those around you. Your self-love literally makes the world a better place! On the flipside, fear of what others think of you and who you "should" be to make them happy holds you back from true self-love and happiness. The good news is there is no need to waste time being afraid of what others think. There is a saying, "When you love yourself, you cannot hurt another." When you have self-love, you radiate love, which attracts all the good in life directly to you.

Ditching Other People's Opinions of You

Love makes the world go around. You may relate to the feeling of butterflies fluttering in your stomach from someone telling you they love you. It feels good to matter to someone we care about. However, most of our feel-good moments ranging from work to parenting come from compliments that are related to our actions pleasing others. Feeling validated and loved by others matters to us too. Contrary to the satisfaction we can feel when we are able to please others, having self-love allows you to remain open to receiving love and validation while making sure your sense of self-worth is not based upon someone else suddenly changing their mind about you. As a result, we are so much stronger and happier when our sense of self-worth is not based upon someone's opinion of us.

Self-love is important and means that regardless of life's ever-changing circumstances, your ability to care about yourself remains intact. Loving yourself prevents you from waiting for someone else to make you complete. You are already complete. When you love yourself, the love you get from others makes your life better without shaking the strong foundation of who you are.

Your inner wild is not only a superpower, but also the greatest middle finger of all time. Whether it is a partner, a family member or boss, if we are not taking care of ourselves our entire day can be shattered by a negative opinion of us. Self-love gives you the strength to understand that regardless of someone else's words or actions, the quality of your life is 100% dependent upon your actions and choices. You have the power to wake up and choose to love and care for yourself each day regardless of others' opinions and whatever life throws at you. You also have the right to choose happiness each day regardless of another person's toxic behavior towards you. You have every right to invest in yourself and live your re-wildest dreams.

Your Inner Wild at Work

You've been warned, your act re-wilding may result in positive change in your life! Positive change naturally happens when we feel great, a beautiful gift we receive when we have love for ourselves. While we learn to re-wild we may decide to make subtle changes that lead to amazing transformational results. When we re-wild we make healthier choices in our life, work, and relationships.

Your inner wild can help you manifest your dream job into a reality or even turn your side gig into a full blown independently owned business. There is a movement happening in today's post-pandemic workplace. Women are beginning to put themselves first. Since the pandemic women are leaving their former jobs in droves and choosing to start their own businesses or take a job that allows them more time for work and life balance. They are refusing to accept less, and it is a wonderful evolution to witness.

Recently I interviewed candidates to replace a consulting position as a writer I was exiting. I posted nationally so the job was opened to candidates all across the U.S. The Covid-19 pandemic was still in full swing. As a result, most of the candidates who applied were women who had to leave their former job to stay home to watch their children while schools shut down during the pandemic. Other candidates had experienced working from home and did not want to return to their former 9 to 5 office environments. I interviewed close to twenty candidates. During the interview I asked the candidates why they were applying for this position, all of the women (and I mean ALL of them) explained the bottom line they were looking to consult online was they did not want to go back to their former jobs. These women were choosing to work on their own terms.

Writing was a dream these women wanted to manifest into a full-time job and their daily reality. I was so impressed by the fact that the women I spoke to refused to accept less moving forward in their lives. They knew they deserved more than their former work circumstances and they went for it. I hope the mass shift for women in the workplace choosing to start their own businesses and working on their own terms continues. We have the power to change the entire future of the workforce if this movement continues.

Ditching the Stress Bully

Stress. There's that dirty word again. Stress is nothing more than a bully on a schoolyard playground. The more stress you have, the more self-care you need to indulge in to relieve your stress. Always remember, self-care is the practice of self-love. You are more powerful than your stress. Part of practicing self-love is to recognize when stress starts to rear its ugly head and to take care of yourself until it goes away. You have the power to choose self-love over stress, but it does require you to care for yourself by doing things that make you feel peace and happiness. Self-love means you no longer put yourself on the back burner. You deserve to do YOU.

I see an amazing life coach and therapist. I am a work in progress. It takes a lot of hard work to recover from PTSD. I am constantly triggered by anything from a sudden loud noise to someone accidentally scaring me. It spins me out for at least a few hours. When I am feeling particularly stressed from life's demands and depleted from anxiety my therapist reminds me to "double down!" on self-care. She reminds me of the importance of practicing self-love like my life depends upon it, and it does. Sometimes I need to triple down! When I start to feel more stress I meditate and pray more, go to the gym, take longer walks in the park, read more, drink more tea, and write in my journal. I make it a point to practice self-care before my house wakes up in the morning.

Self-love also means we no longer allow ourselves to waste our time doing something we don't want to do. When you value yourself you also value your time. One of the most important things we can do as women is to stop overextending ourselves. Listen, Momma! It is ok to buy cookies rather than bake them for your kid's school fundraiser and not feel a damn bit guilty about it. If you feel yourself doing too much, just say NO. Take the time you need for yourself, to be your best self. Be good to you. Your body and mind will thank you.

When we are more relaxed, we are able to reduce our overall stress and the negative effects it can have on our health. Stress can cause your brain to produce increased levels of cortisol and adrenaline leading to increased blood pressure and heart problems. Did you know for up to two hours after feeling a strong emotion like anger you are twice at risk for having a heart attack? Stress also depletes your immune system. The good news is that stress can be significantly reduced by taking just a few minutes each day for yourself.

Assassinating the Superwoman Myth

Do you want to know the secret to doing it all? Don't. Forgive yourself often. Love yourself every moment. Meditate. Pray. Take that nap. Say no. Say yes. Go for a walk and listen to your favorite podcast or music. Allow yourself full permission to spend time by yourself. At the end of the day, good enough is enough.

Even though we live during the 21st century, yet we are still battling the highly outdated, harmful superwoman stereotype of women that has existed for decades, hundreds and even thousands of years. We are forced to compete with the superwoman myth from the moment we wake up to the moment we fall asleep each day. This mythical creature comes in many forms I'm sure you are familiar with. To start with, there are plenty of societal archetypes of the "perfect mom" who works 40-plus hours per week yet amazingly cooks, cleans, and does her entire family's laundry without a hair out of place.

The Superwoman myth is pervasive in social and mass media. It also saturates the advertisements we are exposed to daily. We are constantly being shown commercials featuring only women using cleaning products. Nearly all laundry detergent commercials show women lovingly scrubbing the stains out of their family's clothes. Women are still the ones in commercials making dinner at night. Women are often portrayed as indulging in chocolate or ice cream commercials by themselves, as if eating dessert is something to be ashamed of. Most weight loss advertisements feature and focus on women. Botox and plastic surgery ads primarily target women.

It is easy to see how the superwoman myth is fatal for self-love. It goes directly against your inner wild. The superwoman myth reminds us daily as women we need to do more, that we are never enough and we need to be everything to everyone. Trying to live up to the superwomen hype results in serious burnout. Be brave. Be proud of who YOU are. As women, let's work together to assassinate the superwoman myth by outright rejecting it once and for all. Remember, good enough is enough. When it comes to keeping your sanity, less than good enough is ok too.

Beware the Energy Vampires

I briefly dated a NARC, also referred to as a narcissist. I was twitterpated and he looked great on paper. He was incredibly kind and charming on the first date. After the honeymoon stage of getting to know each other, which was only one week, he was no longer hesitant to show he had a fiery temper, sudden mood changes and was the type of person who yells at a waiter or waitress in a restaurant. During the very short time I wasted dating him, I realized his goal was to control my day based upon his moods and random opinions of me. He fed off of my energy to boost himself up. He was never happy. I was never good enough. No one was. He was an energy vampire. I ran as fast as I could from this negative energy and slayed that energy vampire.

Beware of the energy vampires. They are everywhere. You may be thinking of someone in your life who leaves you emotionally zapped after interacting with them. We have all had that frenemy, partner, family member, boss or coworker who literally sucks the life right out of us. They demand your nonstop attention, and the conversation is always about them. Everything happens to them and it's always someone else's fault. When you try to talk about yourself, they interrupt you and continue to talk about themselves. When you need a shoulder to cry on, they continue to show a lack of empathy and keep the focus on themselves. Dr. Northrup adds that constantly having our energy drained by an energy vampire can have negative effects on "multiple systems in the body, including the immune, cardiovascular, neuroendocrine and central nervous systems." They will suck the self-love right out of you.

    Energy vampires prey on women because we are more afraid to be rude than our male counterparts. They are automatically drawn to those of us who are willing to politely listen. It is ok to say no or politely avoid draining conversations with energy vampires. Dr. Christiane Northrup, author of Dodging Energy Vampires: An Empath's Guide to Evading Relationships That Drain You and Restoring Your Health and Power, explains "What makes energy vampires so toxic is that they can be sources of chronic stress….You're constantly walking on eggshells around that person; waiting for the next shoe to drop."

    You can slay your energy vampires by putting yourself first. One of the benefits of practicing self-love is your ability to spot energy vampires becomes finely tuned. Self-love empowers you to refuse to offer your time to someone who does not value you in return. An effective way to handle an energy vampire is to recognize their behavior and avoid engaging with them in the first place. Trust your intuition. If you feel someone is an energy vampire during a job interview, on a first date or when you meet someone who is negative, set boundaries to ensure they are not allowed to be a stressful presence in your life.

    Energy vampires are often someone we cannot avoid, such as a boss, partner, friend or family member. If you are forced to be around an energy vampire, it is ok to refuse to give them your energy. Dr. Northrup offers advice on being a "gray rock" around an energy vampire meaning you simply refuse to give them the energy they are looking for and they will eventually leave you alone. You can still be a kind and compassionate human being and say no to energy vampires being allowed to suck you dry.

Another way to deal with energy vampires is to outright refuse to accept their behavior. It is better to regret being rude than have your energy sucked out of you because you are too nice. It's ok to be rude. The regret you may feel over being rude takes less time to recover from than sacrificing yourself to an energy vampire.

Growing Your Self-Love

Now that you have learned the importance of self-love as a superpower, make a habit of loving yourself. Self-love grows stronger over time with practice. Even taking a few moments out of your day to sit and appreciate the beauty within yourself can help you begin to experience the many benefits of self-love.

Take a moment to practice reading the following self-love affirmations out loud. I encourage you to surround yourself with their positive energy. One practice I use is to write these self-love affirmations on post-it notes. I stick them on my bathroom mirror, in my car and on my laptop to remind myself of the gifts self-love can bring to help me live my best life on my own terms. Repeat the affirmations as many times as you need to. These words should become a part of you.

> "I deserve to be happy."
> "I accept my true self."
> "I am unique and beautifully imperfect."
> "I love myself exactly where I am at."
> "Perfection is a myth. I am enough."
> "My goal is progress, not perfection."

I hope you enjoy every moment of re-wilding through loving yourself. May you begin each day with self-love. I pray you feel the joy self-love can manifest in your life. Next, you are about to do something very brave. You are going to confront your limiting thoughts and insecurities. You will learn ways you can transform your thoughts into tools to help you live your best life. Together we will explore how meditation and prayer can help you connect with your inner wild to manifest positive growth and happiness in your life.

Chapter 6: Re-Wilding the Buddhish Way

"The goal of meditation isn't to control your thoughts, it's to stop letting them control you." **Anonymous**

Discovering Meditation

I stumbled upon meditation in my twenties while backpacking solo through China. I was on my way to the Shaolin Buddhist monastery near the Songshan mountains in the Henan province. It is believed Shaolin is the birthplace of Buddhism and meditation in China. Built over 1,500-plus years ago in 497 A.D. I was beyond excited to stay at a place so rich in culture and history. During my numerous solo backpacking travel adventures in China, I heard fantastic tales about the Shaolin Buddhist monastery. I met a backpacker who swore up and down that Shaolin was a magical place that could change your life. I can still hear the power of conviction he had while telling me in his German accent, "Shaolin reminds you what matters in life, you know?" That was all I needed to hear. I knew I had to go and witness Shaolin for myself, and it was well worth the extra effort it took to travel through rural China to get there.

My number one rule of traveling alone, especially internationally, is to never venture out at night. At the time, the only way I could get to the Shaolin Buddhist monastery was to take the one shuttle bus available there and it only ran at night. I would need to break my number one travel rule and I would be showing up at Shaolin late that night.

I enjoy meeting locals during my travels. I had nothing but

positive experiences traveling solo through China. The people were always so kind and helpful. If I was stuck on a train platform clearly looking lost, there was always someone who would come and lead me to where I needed to go. Families on my travels loved to practice speaking English with me and I would practice my dodgy Mandarin with them. If I struggled to put my backpack in an overhead compartment on a bus or train, there was always someone who would step in to help me. Living in China reminded me of the importance of always helping others, with even the simplest tasks.

It was a pitch-black night on my way to the monastery. I was in the countryside so there was no light pollution. The stars were brilliantly shining in the sky that night. There was a heavy fog that began to surround the transport van as we drove up a mountain closer to the monastery. The shuttle van had no seats. I sat on the metal floor on top of a spare tire while we bounced along the road. Finally, the van came to a halting stop and the driver told me to "Wai guo ren, xia cha" meaning "Hey foreigner, this is where you get off". I was genuinely scared. I almost stayed in the van, but I honestly didn't know where it would end up that night and if there would be a place for me to stay wherever the van ended up. At the time I was in China, foreigners were only allowed to stay at legally designated hotels and hostels, and I was in a part of central China that few foreigners traveled to at the time.

As I got off the van and stepped out alone into the night. I could only see trees ahead of me. Beyond that was only dense fog. I did not see any buildings, lights, or signs of people. The van quickly screeched away. In my experience, Chinese drivers do not drive slowly. They skillfully haul ass even along the sides of steep mountain roads with drop offs. It almost feels like you are in a video game riding in a taxi or trying to dodge buses, motorcycles and cars coming from all directions as you cross the road.

I felt panic set in as I was entirely alone in the forest in the middle of China. I had no idea where to go. I was thinking I would just have to sit out the night outside when suddenly three petite elderly women stepped through the fog and walked toward me. They did not say a word and kept chatting amongst themselves as two of them wrapped their elbows in mine. They walked me to the monastery and led me to the front desk where I was able to check in safely for the night. I never saw those precious women again for the rest of my stay. I am so grateful they showed up that night. I realized they likely check the van stop for random foreigners like myself who may find themselves feeling lost in the middle of the night on their way to the monastery.

During my stay at Shaolin, I was the only foreigner there. I woke up my first morning at Shaolin to the sound of kung fu drills being performed by children and adults of all ages in perfect synchronicity. Some of the children could not have been more than eight years old. I was fortunate to stay at the Shaolin monastery before it was a heavily visited tourist site and more of a home for orphaned children and teenagers who trained with a shifu, or mentor. I saw the children and adults practicing kung fu with such impressive skill it is difficult to describe. I saw a room full of young men in bright, colorful silk clothing practicing drills with a spiked ball and chain with such intense precision it was incredible. The level of skill there was out of this world.

One of the gifts of travel, and occasionally breaking our own travel rules, is it expands our horizons. My stay at the monastery was a transformational experience for me. My life would never be the same. Shaolin residents are known for waking up at 4 am to meditate for one hour followed by another hour of chanting. The foundation of Shaolin kung fu is a combination of Taoism and Buddhism and meditation is central to their overall practice. Shaolin monks begin the day with meditation to relieve negative thoughts and empower their minds. My days there were filled with meditation. I was deeply inspired by my stay at the monastery to also find my own mind-body connection in my life. Thus began my lifelong journey into mindful meditation.

Meditation: More Than a Trend

Meditation always saves me from my dark side. When I start negative "stinking thinking" I meditate ASAP. Since I began meditation, my mindset has experienced an incredible shift from feeling like a helpless mess at times to being able to reconnect with my inner wild and feel true peace throughout my day.

Meditation is not just a trend. It is becoming more and more mainstream. The Center for Disease Control (CDC) reports meditation is the fastest growing health trend in the U.S. Meditation is quickly gaining a respected position in western medicine as research on the benefits of mindfulness demonstrate its many life changing effects. The goal of this chapter is to explore ways you can form positive thoughts and mindfulness daily to connect with your inner wild to experience more inner peace, joy and success in all areas of your life.

Do you know meditation can make you happy? Now that is a life-changing benefit worth trying out! Research shows regular meditation helps us battle chronic stress and anxiety. When we engage in a regular mindfulness practice, we no longer sweat the small stuff that used to bother us. When we breathe deeply during meditation, we actively calm that pesky, highly reactive, easily triggered fear center lizard area of our brain, the amygdala. Research shows over time an established meditation practice reduces our natural inclination to revert to our survival-focused, reptilian brain. Practicing meditation reduces unnecessary fear and stress in our lives, which makes us happier and healthier.

In addition to increasing our overall health and happiness, scientists are discovering meditation also improves your attention span. As women, we are no strangers to task switching which can often leave us feeling scattered and depleted. Meditation helps us to regain and keep our focus and not be pulled in too many directions. Practicing mindfulness helps us better recognize distractions and remain present so we are not as easily overwhelmed by life's daily adulting tasks.

Meditation provides an effective way to develop self-love and compassion towards others, making the world a better place. The more we meditate the better we will feel, and remember good things come to us when we feel good. The greatest part of meditation is we only need ten minutes a day to experience the life-changing benefits of engaging in a regular mindfulness practice.

When East Meets West

My daughter recently asked me if I meditate or pray. I told her I do both. I explained to her that Eastern mindfulness meditation and the way I learned to pray from Western religion go together for me "like peanut butter and jelly". Although meditation originated in the East, you are not cheating on God if you meditate. I am not a religious expert, but meditation is mentioned throughout the bible. Prayer allows you to talk to your higher power and meditation allows you to listen. If you have a higher power, whatever your higher power may be, you can include prayer with your meditation practice.

Throughout the beginning of recorded history, and even prior to humans meeting other tribes, we know spirituality and forms of prayer and meditation have been present in nearly every culture. Religions and cultures throughout the world have included a form of mindful introspection and contemplation ranging from prayer to sweat lodge ceremonies.

Meditation has been around for thousands of years. Some archaeologists date the beginning of meditation all the way back to 5,000 BCE. That is over 5,000 years before the western world believes Christ was born and 50 centuries before Christianity existed. The practice of meditation spread throughout Asia on the Silk Road. As meditation grew throughout the world it would transform to fit within each culture and religion.

Being Buddhish

My daughter also asked me if I was Buddhist to which I responded, "I guess you can say I am Buddhish". Of all the spiritual beliefs to date, Buddhism firmly practices meditation as the heart and soul of its practice. You may be wondering if Buddhism is a religion. There are many answers to this question depending on where you are in the world, but I will share the Dalai Lama's explanation, "Buddhism does not accept a theory of God, or a creator. According to Buddhism, one's own actions are the creator, ultimately. Some people say that, from a certain angle, Buddhism is not a religion but rather a science of the mind."

You don't have to be Buddhist or have experience with meditation to gain its powerful, life-changing effects. In addition, you also don't need to believe in a higher power to meditate. This is your own personal journey and only you can define how you connect with your greatest inner wild to manifest your greatest happiness. You do what feels comfortable for YOU. I am so excited for you to continue awakening your inner wild!

So far you have learned to connect with your inner wild by practicing your now and zen and taming the big bad wolf by working through your fear. You have learned ways to practice self-love to nurture yourself daily. You are now ready to explore the power of your thoughts to help you further connect with your inner wild to live your life to the fullest.

You Are Your Thoughts

Thoughts are mighty things. You are your thoughts. Please reread that as many times as you need to. Did you know we have more than 60,000 thoughts per day? Scientists estimate that for most people over 80% of their thoughts are negative. Meditation helps us regulate our negative thoughts. It is a powerful weapon against having 48,000 negative thoughts every day of your life.

The saying "Whether you think you can or can't, you're right" is right. We are what we think. If we think we can, we do. If we think we can't, we quit, often before we get started. You now know how to ditch your inner mean girl and stop negative self-talk from sabotaging your happiness and success. But your thoughts go deeper than your inner mean girl thoughts. It is one thing to battle our inner mean girl and quite another when it comes to having a negative mindset on everything outside of yourself as well.

Your thoughts on everything determine the world you choose to live in. Your thoughts are so incredibly powerful that, whether you mean to or not, you manifest the quality, outcomes and even your overall happiness from your thoughts and perceptions. Your process of re-wilding can only occur if you allow it. Your thoughts have a profound effect on your daily moods, changing emotions and even your overall sense of self-worth.

We manifest good in our lives through our thoughts but beware because we can also just as easily manifest the bad. Have you ever held yourself back from going for something you want because of negative thoughts holding you back? You are not alone. Recognizing when negative thoughts are holding you back helps you begin the process of letting them go. Your past is not indicative of your future. We all make bad decisions from time to time. Self-forgiveness is self-love. Allow yourself to be open to all the good you deserve to feel. We are taught throughout our lives it's ok to "settle" and accept our circumstances as they are.

We even have popular sayings in society encouraging us to settle. "Bloom where you are planted" is a good example of a saying we use to try and make the best of our circumstances. The saying, "Bloom where you are planted" is total bullshit. You cannot bloom if you are planted in unhealthy, toxic soil. You need to find a new place to grow. You bloom when you take time to water and nurture yourself. Your inner wild is here to remind you that you do not need to settle for anything in your life that does not make you feel good.

If you work or live in a toxic situation, it's ok to change your circumstances and live your best life. If you find you are struggling with accepting your circumstances as "this is the best it gets", or "I made my bed, now I have to lie in it," and even "I'll never find anyone or anything better" pay attention to why you are questioning if you should "settle" and "accept" your life. You don't need to settle or automatically accept anything that does not serve to make you feel inner peace and joy.

When we feel good, we think good thoughts and good things naturally come to us. One of the most powerful benefits of meditation is we learn to be in tune with our true selves, because when you meditate you meet yourself exactly where you are at. Meditation makes us feel good. It is like you are having a coffee date with yourself where you get to talk to yourself and remind yourself of how much you are worthy of happiness and success in all areas of your life. Meditation allows you to practice self-love by helping you remind yourself you are special and deserving of all things good.

Imposter Syndrome

We are our thoughts, and as women we often don't believe we deserve the success we work so hard to achieve. Have you ever worked your ass off and accomplished your goals, only to feel like you don't deserve to be there? Girlfriend, you are not alone! When we feel imposter syndrome, we feel like we are not good enough to be where we are. Anyone from any background can feel imposter syndrome, but research shows that women feel imposter syndrome more than men. It can be challenging when you are the only woman storming and norming at a job on a team with only men. As women, even when we have shattered glass ceilings and worked five times harder to climb the career ladder, when we finally get a seat at the table many of us feel like we don't belong there. Instead, we continue to doubt ourselves and feel like a fraud.

I learned about imposter syndrome during the first semester of my doctoral program. It was perfect timing because despite my years of academic success, I felt like an imposter having made it into the program in the first place. I was also a nontraditional, first generation, single mom college student who had a baby in her first semester of the program. All new Ed.D. students were required to take a course outlining the logistics of what it takes to complete the four years of mental boot camp ahead.

Our professor kicked off the course by requiring us to read a book by Alfred Lubrano, Limbo: Blue-Collar Roots, White-Collar Dreams. Lubrano shares his story of growing up in a blue-collar household in Brooklyn who went to college and later became a reward-winning journalist. He details the internal conflict many of us feel being raised in a blue-collar world, feeling like we don't fit in when we start working in the white-collar world. What makes this more complicated is that we feel like we don't fit in when we go back home anymore either. We are treated differently by everyone! And it is shocking to realize that our growth is disappointing to some, who are upset that we have changed. Yup...that limbo remains.

Aimee Callahan

I instantly related to Lubrano's imposter syndrome experience being raised in a blue-collar home now living a white-collar life. We moved to Green River, Wyoming when I was in kindergarten because my dad got a job at FMC, a local trona mine. Most people outside of Wyoming have no idea what trona is, but every time you bake with baking powder or baking soda you are actually eating a piece of rock found 1,500 feet underground from a specific part of southwest Wyoming. Trona is a mineral that is mined and is then brought up to the earth's surface where it is processed into soda ash.

Egyptians used soda ash to make glass ornaments and vessels 5,000 years ago. In the 1st century, Romans used soda ash to create everything from glass to medicine. Following in the ancient Egyptians and Romans footsteps, soda ash continues to be processed into everything from baking soda and powder, paper, laundry detergent, toothpaste, medicine to glass. Chances are you use or ingest a little piece of my home state in your home every day.

When you drive through southwest Wyoming on I-80 you see nothing but land for as far as the eye can see. Unbeknownst to most passersby, you are driving over underground cities where trona is being mined. Wyoming supplies about 90% of the world's supply of soda ash with over 1,300 square miles of underground trona deposits. It is estimated the trona reserves in Wyoming will last another 2,000 years. When the mines boomed, so did our little town. We grew into a population of around 10,000 people. The mines pay well. When my dad got the job at the mine our family of five went from living in a single-wide trailer on a piece of land in Eastern Oregon to building our own two-bedroom house with an unfinished basement.

Trona miners work hard. They also work long swing shifts varying their work hours from overnight to working during the day. During the long, dark Wyoming winters, trona miners rarely see the sun because they are underground all day. Trona miners also face danger. The earth is alive at 1,500 feet underground. It is constantly moving and causing the man-made walls of the mine to crack and rocks to fall. Many safety precautions that are nothing short of rigorous are taken, but sometimes the earth wins.

My dad was working on the longwall, the most dangerous part of the mine, and a rock fell and landed on his back. He was seriously injured but alive. He had back surgery and I will never forget the long scar on his lower back. After he recovered he went right back to work. He was never really the same after that accident. It was like something broke inside of him. He was depressed and in pain. My dad died in a skydiving accident not long after his accident at work. I was in junior high. I was that last person in my family to talk to my dad. He had called the night before he died and he told me he was scared to skydive the next day. My dad was a Marine. Later in life he was Airborne in the Army Reserves. He was a highly experienced skydiver. He felt his freest in the sky. I remember telling him to trust his feelings and just not skydive and come home. He then laughed it off and we said our I love you's and goodbyes.

I carried that conversation with me like a heavy weight for decades to come. I wish I had stopped him. My sense of grief and guilt thrashed at my heart and soul for many years. My world was completely spun out when I lost my dad. I felt a pain deeper than my ability to physically cry. All that was left of my dad was buried in three body bags. This pain is still with me today. I know many of you can relate. Losing someone we love is something we never get over, we just learn to live with our never ending grief. Trust me when I say we were far from being an ideal family unit and had our extreme moments of dysfunction, but in spite of that I felt safe and loved with my dad.

As the months went by after his death I would continue to smell his clothes, as his scent made me feel closer to him as if there was a part of him still alive. Eventually his smell disappeared. The scent of Old Spice on his shirts began to smell like dust. I would go places and think for a moment I spotted him from across a room, but it was never him. I had dreams where I could see him in a crowd and I would struggle and push through the crowd to get to him but I never could reach him.

The mine started a summer college hire program for kids of parents who worked there. My mom took a job at the mine after my dad passed away. I took advantage of this opportunity because it was great money. I worked for a summer underground in the trona mine. I would go around with a long metal bar and pull down loose rocks so they would not fall on anyone. I also ran a roof bolter machine. The bolter is a 22-foot long machine with a huge boom at the front. The job of a roof bolter is to drill holes into the freshly mined rock and glue the ceiling and sides to prevent a cave in. There is a lot to it and it is a dirty job. As soon as miners get to the surface, we take showers and put on clean clothes for the 20-mile trip home. But the smell of being covered in the dust from being 1,500 feet underground will forever remain unforgettable to me. Earth dust was the smell I grew up with in Wyoming from smelling my dad's work clothes and later my own.

 I was supervised when I ran the roof bolter. After I could run it alone the boss watched me run the machine to "certify" me on it. That was a very proud moment for me! To that point I was told there were less than five women who ran a roof bolter in that mine. Compared to 95% of men who run roof bolters, only 3% are women. My dad had also worked as a roof bolter. I knew he would be proud. I will never forget how much I appreciated him when I realized how hard he worked for us. He worked a tough, dirty job that wore his body down over time for us. I worked with the same guys who worked with my father for years. I heard them tell crazy stories about my dad. The guys I worked with underground were always talking shit to each other and were experts at practical jokes. They were hilarious. They also took me in and were very kind to me. They were a great crew, and I am so grateful I got to work with them.

 I worked blue-collar jobs to pay for college to live a white-collar life. I glued up rock ceilings 1500 feet underground and later shattered glass ceilings. I have been the only woman on a crew of men working in a mine underground in Wyoming and later in a boardroom with men in positions of power. When I had imposter syndrome, the only person who felt I didn't deserve a seat at the table in the boardroom was me. Over time I have learned that when I face my imposter syndrome and embrace my worth, I find my rightful place doesn't depend upon where I work but how I feel about myself.

Shattering the Glass

As women we have yet to feel naturally entitled for the positions we shatter glass ceilings to fill. We have yet to feel it is our automatic right to be the CEO of a company because the hard truth it still isn't our automatic right. Most CEO positions are still filled by men. A woman usually needs to prove herself as exceptional to earn a position as a CEO. A man just needs to be male.

As women we are still scratching and clawing our way to the top. Multiply this times 100 for women of color. We must work harder to stand out to be considered for most leadership positions. Women still get paid less than men in the same position, 82 cents per their one dollar less to be exact. By the time we get our dream job offer we are so grateful to finally have a seat at the table we often shy away from negotiating our salary to reflect our market value. Never forget to negotiate like a mother fucker.

You deserve to get paid what you are worth. When I am asked what my salary needs are, I have learned to respond by asking what the man was paid who filled the position prior to me. I have taken over two leadership positions where I was hired to come in and organize a neglected department formerly filled by men who spent years doing nothing more than showing up and getting paid. I was grossly underpaid compared to what my worthless predecessors earned, and I had more experience and letters behind my name than they did. I learned the hard way to demand my worth.

I still battle imposter syndrome from time to time but I "check myself before I wreck myself". When I begin to experience self-doubt, I confront my imposter syndrome head on by focusing on valuing myself. Imposter syndrome can spin us out in negative thoughts that can destroy our dreams and hold us back in life. The good news is that we can overcome imposter syndrome and kick it to the curb by taking a moment to reconnect with ourselves through self-love. Never forget this, you deserve to be proud of all you do and accomplish in your life. You also deserve to get paid what you are worth.

Just Breathe!

Having your inner wild silenced can take your breath away,

Aimee Callahan

and not in a good way. Thankfully I have had the opportunity to work with mostly empowering, amazing men and women. I have also had more than my fair share of being "mansplained" in a conference room by the occasional male who felt he was automatically smarter than me simply because he has a penis. You are likely familiar with mansplainers. They only listen to what other men have to say. You know it's not your imagination because they only make direct eye contact with other men in a meeting. They never let you speak. When you do try and speak, you find yourself talking as quickly as possible to say as much as you can before they interrupt you, because they always interrupt you. When you try to get a word in edgewise, they continue to speak over you as if you don't even exist. They love the sound of their voice so much it is oral masturbation for them when they get to hear themselves talk.

Mansplainers are the great silencers of women in the workplace. Being mansplained is a direct attack on our inner wild, and it is maddening. It also supports the imposter syndrome so many of us experience in the workplace. I have gone into many bathroom stalls at work and quietly cried my eyes out after being silenced and ignored by a mansplainer. There have been a few occasions I have been so angry for being silenced it took everything I could to not walk out of the job on the spot. All I could do in these moments was just try not to cry until I got to the bathroom stall... and breathe.

So far in this chapter you have learned about the benefits of meditation as a magical formula for inner peace, but what can you do if you find yourself suddenly in a position where you are feeling overwhelmed, are on display in front of other people and need to feel better immediately like I described above? Just breathe! The importance of mindful breathing cannot be underestimated. When we feel stress, our lizard brain reprograms itself to no longer feel stress, fear or panic when we take deep slow and long deep breaths in and out.

Deep breathing is so simple, and it works within minutes to calm us down. So why don't we breathe when we get upset? First off, we may not know the power of our breath. The power of deep breathing to calm your lizard brain is not something they teach us in school. Secondly, when we feel stress the last thing we are thinking about is breathing. Our brain is literally unable to form a coherent thought. It is in these moments we need to simply breathe more than ever! You can breathe while you are waiting in line at the supermarket. Practice breathing when you are stuck in traffic. You can practice your breathing anywhere. If you choose not to ever meditate, just breathe! Even if you stop reading this book right now, remember to breathe!

Using self-love affirmations also help us to avoid being easily consumed and controlled by our negative thoughts by helping us recognize and release ourselves from the cycle of self-sabotaging thoughts. When you begin to feel the effects of someone's negative behavior creeping in to ruin your day, take a moment to take 10 deep breaths in and out and repeat your self-love affirmations. You can even do this while you are stuck in a meeting with a mansplainer to make the most of your time being stuck with him. There are numerous self-love meditation practices online that help focus your mind and body to feel connected to your inner beauty. With just a little practice we can learn to bring inner peace into life's everyday moments.

The Magic of Letting Shit Go

As grown women we are busy. Getting through some days without losing it can be considered an accomplishment. Adulting can be strenuous. Often, we are exhausted and balancing multiple roles ranging from our careers (many of us have multiple jobs), family responsibilities, relationships with our partners and even our pets. The list goes on and on.

No matter how busy we are, it is completely realistic to set aside at least 10 minutes a day for you to carve out space in your day to relax. A few minutes and a few deep breaths is all it takes to experience inner peace and harmony. Our minds naturally direct us to take breaks. During this time, we tend to turn to social media, surf the internet or marathon a show to veg out. Whether it is early in the morning before everyone is awake, late at night after the world is asleep or a few minutes during the time you would normally spend watching Netflix, take a few minutes every day to allow yourself time for peace and quiet. Tune into yourself and set your vision for the day you want to have. Envision and dream of life you want to experience.

The Dalai Lama said, "Do not let the behavior of others destroy your inner peace." At the end of the day, we may not be able to control how others act, but we can control how we react. Meditation helps you to no longer sweat the small stuff in life that used to upset you. All of a sudden, external circumstance that may have derailed you in the past no longer have control over you. Meditation helps us to be more mindful of the fact that others have no control over how you feel about yourself. You are the one in total control of how you feel regardless of someone else's actions. Meditation is deeply rewarding and meditating for just a few minutes a day can change your life.

How to be a Lazy Meditator

I will be honest with you. I am a lazy meditator, but no matter what I always wake up and do a guided meditation for 10 to 20 minutes. By no means do I meditate like a Buddhist monk. If I sleep in and I am in a rush, I will at least do a 3-minute guided meditation. I don't meditate on my own. I prefer to do guided meditations every morning. I've been meditating regularly for over 20 years, so I can get in the zen zone quickly. I try to sit with my legs in the "criss cross applesauce" position with a straight posture but some days I may do a guided meditation lying in bed before I even lift my head off the pillow. If I cannot sleep at night, I will often play a meditation on my headphones in bed, and it puts me to sleep like a baby. Meditation is a beautiful, blissful escape from our everyday tasks that go directly against celebrating our inner wild. This is how I start my day, every day.

You can accomplish a lot in only a few minutes of meditation. I visualize the kind of day I want to have. I manifest feeling good throughout the day ahead. I breathe deeply and practice my self-love affirmations. I breathe in and out with gratitude for all I have. I thank God for being six feet above ground. I thank the universe for giving me the strength to work through my trauma from the attempted murder.

I focus on surrendering my need to control and overwork myself to my higher power to protect me and guide me towards all the good in the universe. I imagine how amazing it is going to feel when I do my next bucket list. I envision myself facing whatever comes at me that day with grace and compassion for others. I manifest my deepest dreams and desires to live my best life. I set the tone for my day. I embrace my inner wild and it feels great.

There are some mornings I may view meditation like going to the gym and I think I can skip it. Like I said, I can be a lazy meditator. The next thing I know I am getting incredibly agitated in traffic. I am triggered much more easily to feel the negative energy coming my way instead of the positive. I always tell myself when I feel like skipping the gym "the only workout I regret is the one I don't do." I have never regretted going to the gym. The endorphins are healing and the best, natural happy drug we can take. It's the same with skipping meditation. When I meditate regularly traffic does not phase me. It takes a lot to trigger me. Meditating regularly can also help you find inner peace and love on your dark days. During times in my life when I feel intense, overwhelming emotion, like when I am grieving or in a funk I double and triple down on meditation and prayer.

Even though I am a lazy meditator, I still reap the rewards of letting my mind be at peace in less than three to 20 minutes a day. The more time I meditate, the better I feel. I just try and meet myself where I am at. Meditation has saved my mind, body, and soul. I truly do not know where I would be without it. Meditation has given me a greater sense of inner peace, psychological awareness, and mind-body connection. I celebrate my inner wild without abandon when I experience my daily dose of inner bliss through meditation.

Disconnect to Reconnect

Every time you take time for yourself you recalibrate your entire sense of wellbeing. Setting aside precious time for yourself is self-love. Nurturing yourself nurtures your inner wild. Knowing that you are your thoughts, use your time in meditation to think

Aimee Callahan

beautiful, loving thoughts about yourself. There are many guided meditations out there. My go-to which I highly recommend as a total life enhancer is a free 40-day meditation program called Mindfulness Daily by Tara Brach and Jack Kornfield. Whether you are a newbie or experienced meditator they meet you at the beginning of the 40-day journey and guide you through ways you can remain focused during your meditation. Each session is less than 15 minutes long.

You can find Tara Brach's RAIN meditation on YouTube and in less than 12 minutes you can explore exactly where your heart and mind are in this moment and set intentions for peace and happiness in your life. I tend to gravitate toward Tara Brach's meditation programs but there are so many available online. They rock because they meet you where you are especially if you are just starting out. They teach you how to "bring the puppy back" when your mind naturally wanders during meditation. I will literally go through their meditation and choose what I need for the day. I fill my glass back up so I can pour from it.

The time you take to disconnect from the world allows you to reconnect with your inner wild. Your inner wild thrives with meditation! Taking a break for yourself can lead to breakthroughs. It is when we are relaxed and feel good that our greatest ideas and creativity thrives. This is why we see so many world changing ideas come to innovative leaders when they are in the shower or gardening. We are at our most creative when we are relaxed. Taking time to do nothing but be with yourself brings everything into perspective. We see life so much more clearly through our wellness lens. There are over 1,440 minutes in a day, and the good news is meditation is not necessarily about the quantity of time you spend doing it, it is about the quality.

Of course, the more you meditate the more it helps you, but as a busy, single mom I am realistic. I also meditate on the go, and do it wherever I am and whenever I need it. I make it fit into my life. Jennifer Harper-Deacon's 3-minute guided meditation "Re-energising and Reinforcing your Defenses" has grounded me time and time again after having a negative encounter with someone. I have listened to this 3-minute meditation thousands of times. I often take a break from my busy day and do walking meditation. Even though I am in the middle of a busy city filled with sirens and chaos, I take time to soak in all the beauty surrounding me. Everything else can wait because blissing out feels great. Let's take a moment to reflect upon how breathwork and meditation make you feel.

Self-Reflection: Find Your Bliss

Even if you don't do any of the affirmations or exercises in this book, remember to BREATHE. Your practice for this chapter is to remember to breathe when you start to feel stress creeping in. Take at least 5 to 10 deep inhales and exhales. Focus on feeling good. Guess what? You just practiced mindful meditation! Now do this every day.

Just Meditate.

Whether you are a practiced meditator or just starting out, my wellness challenge for you is to meditate. Explore your dreams with your inner wild. Create a mindful space to celebrate yourself. Remember, you don't have to be a practiced Buddhist monk to feel the benefits of meditation. Put your phone on airplane mode-absolutely no texts or social media during this time! Shut off all alerts. You can meditate in silence, play relaxing music or play a guided meditation I recommended here or one you find in an app or online. You can pray while you meditate. Find what works for you, then bliss out. Now do this every day.

I encourage you to journal about how meditating makes you feel. What feelings arose for you during your quiet time? If you don't instantly feel amazing from meditation, don't worry. The positive effects of it sneak up on you. Find a time of day that works best for you to spend at least 10 minutes with yourself and promise yourself you will stick to it. Even if you sit with yourself and think positive thoughts, that is a lot! And when it comes to breathing to help relieve stress all you need to do is remember to breathe more deeply when you start to feel overwhelmed. Your inner wild is waiting for you to zen out. Your bliss awaits!

Next, we are going to explore the reasons why we do a long

list of self-sabotaging, shitty things to ourselves. We will explore ways to harness the power of gratitude to help you manifest your inner wild to heal and overcome treating yourself like shit. You will also learn it is impossible to feel like shit when you feel gratitude.

Chapter 7: How to Stop Treating Yourself like Shit

"My past is an armor I cannot take off, no matter how many times you tell me the war is over." **Jessica Katoff.**

  The toughest battle you will ever fight is the one within yourself. The tougher the battle, the sweeter the victory. We all have our own personal battles. The only person who truly understands your own internal battle is you, making you the only person who can win it. There are times we lose our own battle within. It is during these times we are the hardest on ourselves. We treat ourselves like shit when we cannot handle the pain we feel inside. Sometimes the pain we feel is so great we apply a temporary fix to numb ourselves out. It is human nature to do anything to avoid feeling pain.

  We can be our own worst enemy or our own best friend. It is at the darkest of times you can call upon your inner wild to help you. When life gets to be too much your inner wild is there to lift you up. Re-wilding returns you to your natural, wild state of being. You can use your now and zen as a safe space. Your inner wild will help you double and triple down on self-love to help you work through your pain. Pain has a way of disconnecting us from ourselves, but our inner wild reconnects us.

  The Chinese philosopher Lao Tzu reminds us, "No storm in life lasts forever." Bad moments may not last forever, but they are real and can cut deep. There are days and even months we may feel like we are in a deep, dark funk. Having flashbacks of the Covid-19 pandemic yet? All emotions, even joy, are fleeting but you can establish your inner wild as your home base for positive change and wellbeing. Your now and zen activities and practicing self-love during meditation are a safe space you create for yourself each day. A great meditation is to practice putting a shield around yourself made of golden light that only allows positive energy in.

It is important to "sit in the shit" of our emotions as they arise to work through them. If you are spinning out, take time for yourself or your pain will remain locked inside of you. It is on the darkest of days we need to double and even triple down on our self-love. Working through your painful emotions helps you heal.

Navigating painful moments can make you stronger and yes you CAN do it! Never forget your inner wild is strong as fuck and she is here to help you heal and nurture yourself. Don't be afraid to listen to your emotions. Your emotions are important messengers and their message to you can be life changing. It is often the worst times in our lives that turn out to be our greatest teachers. When you have had enough, your inner wild reminds you of your inner badass. In this chapter you will learn ways to work past your painful emotions. You have the strength to make bold decisions that can lead you to greater happiness and success. Let's get started.

The Trauma Loop

This section is for those of us who have experienced trauma with a big "T" and a little "t" in our lives. It is also for those of you who have not experienced trauma because you are likely close to someone who has. The U. S. Government reports that 50% of women will experience trauma at some point in their lives. If this statistic is true, that means over half of all women are living with trauma. About 8% of women have post-traumatic stress disorder, PTSD. I don't want to confuse trauma with PTSD. Although related, they are two separate conditions. The one thing they both have in common is they can cause us to treat ourselves like shit, so we are going to explore how to navigate not just bad days, but trauma and PTSD with the help of our inner wild.

Although it can feel like it at times, trauma is not a sign of weakness. I always appreciate the Buddhist realistic view of trauma as being something that affects most of us and it is never to be ashamed of nor a personal failure or mistake. Traumatic events are a part of our life story for so many of us. Our inner wild is here to help us heal by activating our bravery, self-love, and compassion.

Trauma rewires our brains to keep us ready to defend ourselves at any moment. Experiencing a traumatic event can trigger your brain to constantly be on high alert. Depending upon the extent of the trauma, you may find yourself feeling easily triggered and on edge due to the fact your brain still thinks you are a cavewoman and thinks you may need to run from a saber tooth tiger at any moment. Our brains have not evolved to realize we don't need to constantly be on the run to survive. PTSD takes this to the extreme. The result is that although we are alive, due to the fact our brains are rewired differently than before, there isn't much of a life living with PTSD. You cannot reach REM sleep, our deep rapid eye movement sleep, which is essential for your overall health and wellbeing. REM is too deep of a sleep for PTSD, you're not safe. PTSD is exhausting.

After the attempted murder, I learned what it was like to live with PTSD. I can only compare having PTSD to living in a horror movie every day, only to wake up and relive it again the next day. It is absolute hell. I don't watch horror movies because I live in one. PTSD won't stop replaying the horror of the attempted murder. PTSD is a trauma loop that replays again and again.

Due to now living with PTSD the parts of me that allowed myself to trust and love a partner romantically became numb. The realization that I would never be the same person I was before that night hit me hard. Now every time I heard a sudden sound, even as simple as a car door slam while walking around the city, I would automatically have flashbacks and go into a panic attack. My deep emotions froze. I could no longer cry. I was emotionally constipated. I did not cry for over a decade unless it was related to a panic attack. Parts of me were dead inside. My self-love was also suffering. It was hard to love myself knowing someone hated me enough to want me dead.

PTSD nightmares don't just replay traumatic events in your mind, they replay it in your entire body too. For two years I did my best to fight off sleep. The moment I fell asleep I relived the attempted murder in excruciating detail. I would wake up flying out of bed covered in sweat, heart pounding, adrenaline rushing ready to fight for my life. This is what I had to look forward to all night, every night. My mind would not allow me to just sleep. I was stuck in a loop of reliving that night repeatedly. I needed to recover and remove the power the attempted murder had over my happiness and wellbeing.

The worst part of experiencing trauma is since your brain is rewired to replay your trauma loop upon even the slightest trigger, and we cannot control outside triggers, and we cannot control our brains' automatic response to triggers. This is a major reason why PTSD is so debilitating and steals your life from you. You are forced to relive what happened to you no matter how much you don't want to. Until we do some serious work, those of us affected by certain traumatic events are stuck in a trauma loop.

Healing from Trauma

If you suffer from trauma, I highly encourage you to work with a trauma trained therapist to help you heal. Therapy has helped me, and is still helping me, work through my PTSD. I have discovered using my voice has been incredibly liberating. However, we now know talk therapy doesn't help heal PTSD because our brains are rewired after traumatic events. I really want to emphasize the point that talk therapy does not heal trauma. You need to find a specially trained trauma therapist who knows how to rewire your brain through brain activation techniques such as EMDR and brain spotting.

Finding the right therapist for you can be absolutely the most empowering, healing action you can take to work past trauma and PTSD. It took me more than a few therapists to find the right one for me. Therapy is expensive and most therapists, in my experience, only take cash and ask you to have your insurance company reimburse you. Take your investment in yourself seriously. Make sure each therapy session is helping you do the work to heal.

My inner wild has given me the courage to take my life

back. My therapist is an empowered woman who dedicates her practice to helping women and moms "UNperfect" (her term) themselves. She calls me out on my bullshit, and she has the knowledge to help my neuroplastic brain heal from trauma. The best way to counteract trauma is to convince, or rewire, our brains to stop overprotecting us. I do brain spotting work with my current therapist to counteract my PTSD triggers. It is hard work. After a brain spotting session I will need to sleep for a few hours. It wipes me out, but each session has literally changed my brain and has helped me heal on a life-changing level. Triggers that used to instantly spin me out are now disappearing from my life.

No matter how hard you try to let go of a past trauma, sometimes your trauma won't let go of you. Before I found my kick ass therapist, I coped with the horror movie that now was inside of my mind like a lot of people with past trauma and PTSD do, I treated myself like shit by misusing alcohol. Many of us turn to trauma blocking behaviors to avoid our pain.

Trauma Blocking

I could not decide whether to call this section Trauma Blocking or Sex, Drugs and Rock & Roll. I went with trauma blocking to cover all the methods we use to treat ourselves like shit in an effort to avoid feeling like shit. The Gottman Institute defines trauma blocking as, "an effort to block out and overwhelm residual painful feelings due to trauma." Trauma blocking is essentially our way of running from feelings that eat us up inside. Trauma blocking is often compulsive. We numb ourselves to avoid our pain, but the relief is temporary.

It is fun to imbibe and catch a lovely buzz to celebrate your day. I am a huge fan of plant-based highs. I am far from the morality police when it comes to having fun. It's when we begin to use our buzz to block and self-medicate our pain that we need to be careful. Trauma blocking behaviors can often result in long-term negative consequences for us. As women, we need to be made aware of the ways we are targeted for mass numbing and taming. America has a long history of drugging women to keep us domesticated and compliant. When it became unethical for men to commit their wife to a sanitarium and marry a younger version of her at the end of the 1800's, the medical system run by the men at the time began to normalize drugging women to keep them well behaved. In the 1800's doctors prescribed morphine and opium to women. By the end of the 19th century, two out of three morphine and opium addicts were women.

After WWII when men came home and women left the workplace and reentered their domesticated life as the quintessential 1950's housewife, doctors prescribed Valium to numb women out to better accept the mundane existence of their everyday lives. Valium was called "mother's little helper" and it was prescribed to women twice as much as men. Women never set out to get addicted, they were just following doctor's orders. Since print media began, advertising has reinforced the mass taming of women through drugs and alcohol, making it normal and sexy for mommies to get fucked up into submission. If women were feeling unhappy it was likely due to living unfulfilled lives. Unhappiness and depression are symptoms of being forced to cage your inner wild. History keeps repeating itself by showing it is better to drug women than let us be wild and free.

After the attempted murder, when I put Chloe to bed it was wine o'clock for me. Due to my lack of sleep from PTSD, I was feeling like a total zombie. I had various sleep aids and numbing prescription drugs prescribed to me by my doctor and yet none of them worked. I remember waking up with a prescription drug hangover and my head would be in a fog. PTSD had officially taken over my life, and I was unable to sleep. No matter how hard we try to numb our intense emotional pain, PTSD is persistent. The flashbacks, lucid nightmares, and panic attacks didn't stop. Even a small reprieve from this with the help of a wine buzz felt like a vacation.

I fell into the trap of thinking it was ok, cute and even a little glamorous, for me to drink too much wine. I desperately needed to feel a sense of relief and sleep. That's what we women do, right? It wasn't like I was drinking too much whiskey. It was just wine. According to social and mass media, all the cool, hip moms drink wine. There are even t-shirts that show how funny and cute it is for moms to cope with motherhood by drinking wine. I began to take it too far. I began to need wine. Every time I had a PTSD episode, I needed wine to numb me out. Soon wine wasn't enough. I needed a few shots to go with it. I fell into a downward spiral of alcohol misuse.

I was drinking jet fuel to self-medicate myself. Not only do we drink ethyl alcohol disguised as sexy beverages, when we drink, we are ingesting a component of gasoline used for our cars. Alcohol is also a serious depressant, which means too much of it does the opposite of making you feel good. Alcohol leaves you with "hangxiety", a term used to describe the extra amount of anxiety you feel the day after drinking too much. Too much alcohol leaves you feeling like shit physically and mentally. If you Google the negative effects of alcohol the list is almost endless.

I was self-destructing by my alcohol misuse. I was no longer a social drinker. I prefer to not drink in social settings. I didn't drink every day. I could go for months without drinking, but the moment I spun out from a PTSD episode I instantly sought to numb myself. I used alcohol to try and block my trauma and it terrified me. I was tired of treating myself like shit, so I stopped misusing alcohol altogether and I immersed myself into trauma therapy. Drinks at a party now have a different meaning for me. I see alcohol as glamorized jet fuel. I don't want in my body.

Trauma blocking, or the ways we treat ourselves like shit, comes in many forms. Regardless of our differing life experiences, we all feel an aversion to pain and some of us may apply distracting behaviors to help us get out of painful moments that feel too heavy to bear. The Gottman Institute lists just a few of the ways we try to avoid intense emotional suffering:
- Binge drinking every weekend because you are off from work
- Excessive and mindless eating even when you are not hungry
- Becoming a workaholic and having poor boundaries at work including being available 24/7
- Compulsive exercising to reach a goal you are never satisfied with
- Being uncomfortable being alone
- Staying in toxic relationships long after their expiration date
- The feeling of being uncomfortable if you have nothing to do and the need to always have projects to do

- Excessive use of social media and compulsive mindless scrolling
- Compulsive online shopping for things you do not need and going into debt

Do any of these feel familiar to you? The list is missing using compulsive sex and other behaviors we use to distract us from our pain. Please feel free to ask me about most of the above trauma blocking behaviors as I have earned a few gold medals from the above list! Before trauma therapy, you name it. I've done it. I understand this behavior intimately as I have been very, very good at avoiding my pain. For too many years I chose to self-destruct and sacrifice my wellbeing rather than face my intense emotional suffering. The above behaviors are but a few that we use to mask our pain.

At the time of the attempted murder, I was teaching a Public Speaking class at a local community college in Laramie, Wyoming. The incident had been in the local newspaper and thankfully my daughter's and my names were not reported. Being a small town, the news was everywhere. I overheard a few of my students talking about what they had read in the newspaper and one of my students simply stated, "Why didn't she just shoot him?" This is considered a common response in a small town in Wyoming where gun culture is prevalent in a hunting community.

Why do we still blame women for being attacked in society? I thought to myself, "Why didn't my attacker choose not to try and kill me?" Why was it my responsibility to "stop" him rather than him not break in my front door in the first place? The comment hung in my mind for some time. I can confirm the circumstances of how that night played out would have made it very difficult for me to have defended myself with a firearm, even if I had one. When you wake up with a dark figure standing over you in bed you just don't have enough time to react the way you wish you could. All you can do is fight like hell and try to run.

There is a quote from Buddha that says, "Anger is like drinking poison and expecting the other person to die." I was filled with so much anger for years after the attempted murder. I finally learned how to forgive my attacker on my own terms to release myself from the power his actions had over me. As long as I was angry inside, that night owned me. I was sick and tired of being tired, so I took my own power back.

Over time I was able to stop focusing on my anger and hurt and chose to focus on self-love and gratitude. I reminded myself each day above ground was a gift and I was grateful to be able to live life to the fullest. When I was free from negativity, I was free to be my true self. Opportunities began to open up to me in amazing ways. Within just two years I accepted a job position I had previously thought would take me at least ten years to achieve. Eventually I did begin to live my life to the fullest again. I also trained to defend myself. Learning how to protect myself has been another source of healing for me.

I take whatever measures I need to feel safe. Two months afterwards my daughter and I moved to Denver. I moved us into a high rise with around the clock security. For much of her childhood, I have raised my daughter in a highly secure downtown high rise with cameras everywhere and 24/7 security onsite. I will never again live or sleep in a house where my bedroom is near the front door.

If you are a trauma survivor, please know you are not alone. Half of us are going through a similar process of learning how to live with something that has deeply affected us. If you have not experienced trauma, thank you in advance for loving us and supporting those of us who are learning to navigate our way towards wellness.

No matter what happens to you, your inner wild is still intact. Your inner wild can offer a safe, healthy way to help you stop treating yourself like shit. When you re-wild, you do things that are good for you. When you feel good, you naturally attract more good into your life. Trust your inner wild to give you the courage you need to heal. Never doubt how brave you are. You deserve to live a life filled with delightful inner peace and outside joy. Despite all we may do to block our intense emotional pain, our body and mind continues to try and process the pain. Pain always bubbles to the surface. The best way to truly be free of our trauma is to not only do therapy but to learn ways to feel good on a daily basis. The good news is we can face our trauma in a productive, positive way that fosters self-love for ourselves and compassion for others. The healing process from trauma and negative life experiences can feel good. It doesn't have to be a scary process. We can begin by using gratitude as a positive way to feel joy every day. Gratitude works as a highly effective trauma blocking behavior you can use anywhere at any time!

Gratitude Brings Peace

Melody Beattie, author of Codependent No More, reminds us that gratitude, "...makes sense of our past, brings peace for today, and creates a vision for tomorrow." It took me years to realize that although I would never be who I was before the attempted murder, and that is ok. I am grateful I survived. I can heal and evolve into someone better. It has been a long journey of over a decade so far, but I must take what happened that night and do something positive with it. Rather than wish that night never happened, I am grateful for the strength it has given me to re-wild into living the best version of myself I have met so far! I have turned my pain into purpose. Since I began my journey toward healing, I have resolved to dedicate my life to helping other women re-wild.

An attitude of gratitude is pure magic for all of us. Whether you are having a bad moment or a bad day, gratitude can help you feel better. Gratitude is emotional intelligence in the purest form. Being grateful is good for you. When you feel gratitude, you feel greater happiness and positivity. Gratitude increases our capacity for self-love and compassion for ourselves and others. Gratitude transforms us into a magnet for positive energy, positive people, and more opportunity. Gratitude erases negativity. It is impossible to feel resentment and bitterness when we feel grateful.

When we express our gratitude, even for the small things in life, research shows our happiness increases by over 25%. Research also shows that an attitude of gratitude can help you sleep better at night. Studies have also shown that gratitude can help increase your patience to help you make better decisions. Gratitude deepens your relationships. Gratitude is a simple act you can practice daily with amazing results.

Toxic Positivity-Don't Fake It Until You Make It

None of us feel amazing all the time. If you feel like shit, it's ok to listen to the message your emotions are sending you. Your inner wild will always signal you when something is not right. Maybe something in your life needs to change. If you need to feel like shit, allow yourself time to feel all the feels. Then allow yourself the time you need to feel better.

When I feel like a toddler that wants to cry and melt down in public, I try to double down on taking some time to myself for some self-love. I will usually lie down and zone out on a guided meditation that helps me focus on what I need most, which is usually a feeling of gratitude. I let myself relax. I cuddle with my dachshund. When I take a nap, I feel like I am wrapped in a safe cocoon. I give myself permission to completely unwind and reconnect with my inner wild. Your inner wild is always here to remind you of how wonderful and unique you are. Tuning into your inner wild helps you reconnect with feeling good.

As much as I appreciate the saying "fake it until you make it," it is ok to feel like shit sometimes. Rather than treat yourself like shit during these moments, tap into your inner wild for support. Drop everything if you need to. Do your now and zen. Lie down and meditate. Cuddle with your pets. Go for a walk and take deep breaths to ground yourself in wellness. Be kind to yourself when you feel like shit.

The other day I had a friend ask me, "How do you stay so positive?" I told her I have those days where I struggle, but I also know those days will end. No matter how bad a day is I am glad to be alive to feel like shit. I then asked her if I was being annoying by trying to always be positive because the last thing I want to do is bring toxic positivity to those I love.

Toxic positivity is the idea that no matter how traumatic your circumstances may be, you should be positive no matter what. Saying things to those in pain like, "Other people have it worse" or "don't be sad, that will just make it worse" are examples of toxic positivity. Rather than validate our feelings, forcing away the truth of our feelings by a false smile does not help us to heal our mind, body, and soul. Toxic positivity is toxic. It makes us feel even worse for not being ok. It takes away our right to feel like shit.

I tend to be a happy person and practice all we are discussing in this book, but I definitely understand the darker side of some days. Sometimes the best thing about certain days is knowing that, like storms in nature, they will end. The sun always rises again tomorrow. Mother nature gives us a chance to reset each day. We are here to embrace our true selves, not force them to act unnaturally. I understand how easy it is to get caught up in our own negative thinking. I try to keep my glass half full, but I am human. Re-wilding does not mean we need to pretend or force ourselves to be happy all day. The process of re-wilding allows you to be all you are on the good days and days that are more challenging.

Gratitude is the Law of Attraction

The beauty of gratitude is that it is all or nothing! Negativity simply cannot exist in the same presence as gratitude. You may have heard of the power of the universal law of attraction. I absolutely believe gratitude is the best way to work the law of attraction in our lives. Jack Canfield, author of multiple best-selling books on the law of attraction and the Chicken Soup for the Soul series, explains, "The Law of Attraction states that whatever you focus on, think about, read about, and talk about intensely, you're going to attract more of into your life."

You can grow your own garden of gratitude. DO stop and smell the flowers in your garden of gratitude by making a habit of celebrating all of the small things in your life you are grateful for. We can reside along the spectrum of negative to positive depending on the day and our stress triggers. However, practicing gratitude can become a habit that has the power to change your outlook on life. Simply put, when we practice gratitude, we welcome not only happiness but abundance into our lives. Oprah reminds us, "Be thankful for what you have; you'll end up having more. If you concentrate on what you don't have, you will never, ever have enough." When we focus on feeling grateful for what we have, it fills us up.

With a grateful mind you are better able to recognize and even create opportunities for positive change and success in your life. Even while I was going through the darkness of my trauma, what I was most thankful for in my life grew exponentially. Gratitude helps us stop pursuing the things we don't have and instead feel grateful for what we do have. So, what do we do when we have weeds in our garden of gratitude? Start by not letting them overrun your garden. It is ok to have bad moments and even bad days. These are the annoying little weeds in your garden.

Joel Osteen makes an excellent point when he stated, "You cannot hang out with negative people and expect to have a positive life." My mom had a similar saying that really hit home for me, "If you wade knee deep in shit some of it is going to rub off on you." Ever notice how when you hang around someone who is constantly negative, or you are the negative one, it really can ruin a good time and affects not only your mood but everyone around you? On the flipside of this coin, have you also noticed how when you are the positive one, or around someone who chooses to be positive, that good energy is contagious?

Focus on growing your flowers and the weeds will likely disappear over time. If there is a persistent weed in your garden, it may need to be pulled. For example, if you are unhappy working for a toxic boss and it is affecting your overall mental, spiritual, and physical wellbeing it might be time to look for another job. You can grow and change your garden as you see fit just like you can make positive changes in your life to remove situations that affect you in a negative way. If you don't like it, you have the power to change it. Your inner wild roars with delight when you change that which does not serve your greater good.

The Gift of Gratitude

Anyone can learn to practice gratitude. Gratitude is a mindset and there are simple practices that can help you begin to experience all the good gratitude can bring you. A great way to start practicing gratitude is by making a gratitude list. You can keep a running gratitude list in your re-wilding journal. There are gratitude apps you can download that send you daily gratitude prompts when you wake up and before you go to sleep. Most of the apps send you daily quotes and positive affirmations. A gratitude journal is also great to look back on when you need a pick-me-up on those tough days. When you take a few minutes to write down your gratitude list for the day it helps solidify the benefits gratitude can bring you. Over time, you will see your list of what you are grateful for change and grow in positive ways as you attract more good into your life.

Another way to practice gratitude is to share gratitude daily with family, friends, coworkers and even strangers. When you thank others for even the simplest of acts it helps you and others feel good. The gift of gratitude helps make the world a better place. You can share a daily gratitude text with friends and family. There are also gratitude challenges you can participate in.

Will Bowen, author of the book A Complaint Free World: How to Stop Complaining and Start Enjoying the Life You Always Wanted, created the 21-day complaint free challenge that has been used by millions around the world. The goal is to go at least 21 days without complaining to practice a gratitude lifestyle. It is simple but challenging. You start by wearing a purple rubber bracelet. When you complain you put the bracelet on the other hand and need to start over. Bowen is the first to admit it took him six months to go 21 days without complaining. This is a fun challenge you can do solo or recruit others to join you. When sharing your daily gratitude with your friends and family you can also ask them to share what they are also grateful for. You can pay the gift of gratitude forward by creating a gratitude community. You can learn to rely on each other on days you could use a positive boost.

Gratitude Listing

Let's do a simple fast exercise. Writing a quick gratitude list every day keeps the negative away!

Take out your re-wilding journal, download a gratitude app, or use a scratch piece of paper or post-it note. Write "I am grateful for..." at the top. List at least five things you are grateful for. Be spontaneous. There are no right or wrong answers. You can list

The Re-Wilding of Womxn: Chapter 7

small things and big things you are grateful for.

That's it! You're done!

I encourage you to do daily gratitude lists. This simple exercise can bring you a greater sense of happiness and wellbeing. You deserve to feel good every day!

Now that you have learned to attract what you want in your life with gratitude, you are ready for even more greatness to come your way. You didn't come this far to only come this far! Babes, it's long overdue we proudly turn the lights on during sex. A shocking majority of women suffer from being uncomfortable with their body image. It's time to start a worldwide sisterhood of acceptance and support for one another where we feel safe to express our bodies on our own terms, according to our own personal values. In the next chapter you are going to begin the journey of re-wilding your ASSets.

Chapter 8: Re-Wilding your ASSets

"Treat your body like it belongs to somebody you love." - Anonymous

The Pandemic of Female Body Image Distress

If you struggle with loving your body image, you are not alone. Over 91% of women state they do not feel comfortable with their body image. The National Eating Disorders Collaboration defines body image as "...the perception that a person has of their physical self and the thoughts and feelings that result from that perception." Notice how the definition of body image is all about how you feel about your body, not about how you look. Research studies from Stanford University and the University of Massachusetts report over 70% of college women say they feel worse about their own looks after seeing women in magazines and mass media. Only 5% of women naturally possess the ideal body image constantly displayed in social and mass media. It is a devastating fact that the vast majority of us don't like the way our bodies look.

The fact that only 9% of us feel comfortable with our bodies is what I refer to as the pandemic of female body image distress. Loving the bodies we are in affects our relationship with ourselves and with others, because how we see ourselves in our own bodies directly affects our ability to love ourselves and our partners. Research shows having a negative body image can put us at greater risk of low self-esteem, anxiety, depression and eating disorders. Not being comfortable with our bodies can also affect our ability to engage in emotional and sexual intimacy in our relationships.

Our inner wild comes in all shapes and sizes. Your inner wild is directly linked to our appreciation of who you are inside and on the outside. Like a snowflake glistening in the sun floating through the air on a cold winter day, there is only one YOU. Congratulations on being one-of-a-kind! You deserve to love yourself and the body you are in. It is your right to wake up every day and feel sexy. Your inner wild is here to remind you that you already are the ideal woman, because there is only one wildly unique you.

This chapter is dedicated to helping you re-wild your AS-Sets. We are going on a journey to empower our love for our bodies. You are going to learn to recognize the ways social and mass media constantly train you to reject the love you should have for your YOUnique body. You will be able to call bullshit on unrealistic, airbrushed images of women displayed in social and mass media as being the norm of what you "should" look like. We are going to learn how to take our bodies back! At the end of this chapter, you will practice ways you can re-wild by celebrating and connecting with your unique body.

Re-Wilding the Big Lie

The big lie of what the ideal female should look like throughout history in nearly all societies is an ironic, cruel joke on women. The big lie has incredible power over our ability to love the bodies we are in. As women we are reminded and taught to feel insignificant and reject our own bodies if we do not look like the 5% of women on display in social and mass media. We quickly forget that even the 5% of women on display are airbrushed to the extent that even these perfect unicorns don't look like their dramatically altered photos in real life. Do the 5% really exist at all, especially after the age of 25? The big lie maintains we should look like a nonexistent woman.

The tragedy of the big lie is that we are so inundated by these false images of what our bodies should look like, we forget to love the body we have. You only have one body in this life, but social and mass media teaches us our unique bodies do not matter unless they look like the nonexistent woman. The powers that be that flaunt the nonexistent woman in your face do not care if you love your body. In fact, the less you love your body, the more money they can make off you. We see a vast array of beauty advertisements aimed at women urging us to emulate the nonexistent woman. As a result, we see plastic surgeons. We get ass implants. We have our fat frozen and sucked out of our beautiful thick thighs. We over inflate our lips. We try to emulate a Kardashian if they put a photo on display of their thigh gap by a pool. Even though many of us see these images as ridiculous we cannot help but feel influenced by them in negative ways.

The pandemic of female body image distress is a topic that is near and dear to me as growing up I had deep, internal struggles with my own body image. Why did I need to feel like my body needed to look a certain way to fit into society? Why didn't I recognize the big lie I was supposed to look like the unrealistic archetype of the nonexistent woman? Because those are the images, I was inundated with from mass media and I subconsciously compared myself to that ideal.

As a teenager I filled out at a young age and was very curvy. I didn't look anything like the teenage girls in my magazines. All of the girls in my magazines were white and had thigh gaps. I filled out at a young age, and I had bangin curves, but this was before girls with booties were celebrated like they are now. One advantage of looking like a woman at 16 was that I could buy alcohol without getting ID'd. I tortured myself needlessly by trying to fit the latest image of what the "perfect" girls looked like.

I have starved myself. I have stuck my fingers down my throat and prayed to the porcelain gods to make me skinny. Since the moment I hit puberty, I have felt uncomfortable with my body image, and I would constantly compare myself to the nonexistent women I saw on television and billboards. For as long as I can remember, I have equated my sense of self-worth to my jean size. If this thought process sounds familiar to you, keep reading because we are going to learn how to take our bodies back from the nonexistent woman we are held up to by social and mass media.

The Unbecoming

The nonexistent woman is unavoidable. We are surrounded by her image in social and mass media from the moment we wake up to the moment we go to sleep. There is simply no avoiding the image of the nonexistent woman. She is the queen of mass media. She has been around since the beginning of organized civilization and her body morphs over time. The nonexistent woman has been depicted in cultures around the world since the beginning of recorded art history. Her duty has been to represent her husband's status in both her behavior and appearance. Her slender, curve less image can be found in ancient Egyptian art. She was the plump, large breasted woman in Greco-Roman culture. She is the full-bodied woman represented in the art of the Italian Renaissance. She is the tightly corseted Victorian woman celebrated for her tiny waist. She is the movie star with the hourglass figure during the golden age of Hollywood. She then evolved into the rail thin heroin chic of the 1990's. She is the postmodern beauty of today expected to have a tiny waist but a big butt, but not too big of a butt, large breasts, but not too large, a flat stomach and a thigh gap.

The nonexistent woman is a direct assault on our inner wild. Her job is to keep women feeling insignificant about themselves and she is very good at her job. She ensures we feel we are not worthy enough of love unless we look like her. She trains us to think we need to look like her to be happy in life. Rather than celebrate our unique bodies, we are forced to have the nonexistent woman shoved in our face all day, every day of our lives. She stares at us from glossy magazine covers we see while waiting in line at the supermarket. She is on the billboards surrounding us while we are stuck in traffic. She is in pop up advertisements online and in nearly every television show and movie we watch. She is everywhere. She also models our clothes, lingerie, and swimming suits for us, making it hard for us to shop knowing how much our bodies will not look like hers when that bikini arrives.

When I was an undergraduate student at the University of Wyoming, I took a class taught by Dr. Debra Beck (may she

R.I.P.), called Women in the Media. This class changed my life and would later influence my graduate studies. Dr. Beck's class made my mind explode. It was not until I took this class in college that I realized the manufactured truth behind the images of women in mass media. That summer I underwent a major Unbecoming. I re-wilded my love of my body. I stopped falling into the trap of thinking I needed to look like the nonexistent woman in social and mass media. The stark realization that most media images do not portray real, empowered women, but rather focus on the superwoman myth of being perfect, was a completely transformational learning experience for me. Never again would I see women on magazines and billboards the same way ever again. The archetype of the nonexistent woman in social and mass media lost its power over me.

Unbecoming what society has defined we "should look" and embracing our inner wild begins with awareness. In order to re-wild our assets, it is important to understand how our bodies have been used by controlling forces in society to control and tame us over time. As we navigate our inner wild, it is important to recognize the daily messages we are given that work to train and subdue us as women. The more we feel we are not living up to the nonexistent woman, the easier it is to control us. The nonexistent woman kills our inner wild.

Seeing through the bullshit of the nonexistent woman is a powerful act of re-wilding. Being force fed images that are meant to prevent us as women from loving the bodies we are in goes directly against the spiritual, psychological, and physical benefits of re-wilding. It is time we revolt against the images of women in mass media that depict us as tiny, weak, submissive women. We as women have the power to see through social and mass media lies and openly refuse to accept how we are inaccurately portrayed.

Not only is it time to reject these fake, controlling images of women as being an ideal we should live up to in society, but we need to keep a critical eye on all social and mass media messages. The other day I was at a store and on the cover of a magazine was the bold headline in bright yellow branding a freshly divorced female movie star as "Desperate and Single!" Other gossip magazines had pictures of famous women's bodies on the beach and had arrows pointing to their cellulite. This is not only tasteless, it is cruel. Women deserve better. When we refuse to accept the invasive, negative narrative of women in mass media we take back our control.

Our body identity is closely related to our sexual wellness, which is heavily influenced by images of submissive, hypersexualized women in social and mass media. Rather than being displayed as women in a position of power, women in social and mass media are often displayed in contorted, weak, and vulnerable positions. We are inundated with images of hypersexualized, nonexistent women in social and mass media selling everything from tires to hamburgers. Even if we try to avoid social and mass media (and we should where it is healthy for us), we still see images of women everywhere reinforcing subjugated images of women according to outdated societal norms.

We celebrate the male "silver fox" in media and movies but as soon as women reach a certain age, they are made invisible in society. Unless an older woman is a "cougar" she is not displayed as "sexy" in the media. We show incessant images of objectified women in mass media in stark contrast to the images we see of fully clothed men in powerful poses. What makes this phenomenon more impactful is that it is not just us who are affected by these mythical images of women. Men, young boys, and young women also see these messages and feel this is the norm for women in society.

It is long overdue that we as women start a proactive re-wilding revolution when it comes to loving our bodies. The nonexistent woman tries to hijack our self-worth. Don't let her have power over you. Use your inner wild and reclaim your right to love yourself right where you are. Learning how drastically we are misrepresented and subconsciously controlled by inaccurate images of women in social and mass media is the first step in breaking free of the power it can have over how we feel about ourselves and our bodies.

F!*k Perfectionism

Succumbing to the pressure to be perfect locks up our inner wild and throws away the key. As women we have a lot of pressure in society to be the perfect everything. The big lie works to oppress our inner wild. We have learned the Superwoman myth is an impossible ideal to live up to, yet we still feel pressure as women to be the perfect mother, wife, partner, sister, daughter, friend and be a size two while doing it, and don't forget to smile! Perfectionism sabotages our inner wild. Not only do we deny our true selves, but we also block our opportunity to experience true happiness.

Due to the pressure put on us to fulfill the cookie cutter (no pun intended) female stereotypes in society and work, women are far more likely to feel the need to be perfect than men. As a result, women also experience far more self-doubt. As women we still suffer from a sense of self-doubt and push ourselves so hard to be perfect, we often forget our true selves along the way. Perfectionism is not only impossible, but also a mental prison put on women by societal forces who benefit from controlling us.

Striving for the fallacy of perfectionism automatically places us in a position to seek external approval, to be ranked, filed, and judged by others. It is a powerful act of re-wilding to not base your happiness on what others may think of you. Our inner wild automatically takes a backseat when we strive to be the nonexistent woman. All we need to be for ourselves is already who we are. Self-love is a superpower and loving yourself based upon your own terms can make you experience greater life satisfaction, physical wellbeing, and overall happiness.

Let me just start by saying, f!*k these stereotypes. As women we are all better off revisiting the negative influence these stereotypes have on our overall happiness and wellbeing. They subconsciously infect our minds and poison our self-esteem. None of us are perfect and thank goodness for that. Imagine how boring it would be to spend a day with someone who is perfect. I have never met anyone who is perfect, and I am grateful for that. We all have our own unique, delightful imperfections that make us special.

Wabi-Sabi

Leonard Cohen reminds us, "There is a crack in everything. That is how the light gets in." The Japanese view of wabi-sabi celebrates imperfection in beauty as being the most beautiful, unique aesthetic of all. Rooted in Zen Buddhism, wabi-sabi is the beauty of all things unconventional. Wabi-sabi notices and celebrates traits that are not defined as typically being beautiful, finding beauty in imperfection.

Beth Kempton, author of, Wabi Sabi, a Japanese Wisdom for a Perfect Imperfect Life, explains, "Put simply, wabi sabi gives you permission to be yourself." When we recognize wabi-sabi we see the beauty in what makes us unique. Wabi-sabi allows us to meet our inner wild right where we are at and recognize our imperfections as absolutely perfect.

Thankfully, through the years I have realized the scale can be a dirty, filthy liar. Take your scale and throw it out the window. A scale does not measure your worth. My motto now when it comes to my body is "nourish to flourish." I refuse to starve myself ever again. I refuse to stick my fingers down my throat. Once I became aware of how images of women in the media influence us to be hard on our bodies, I learned to eat healthy and exercise in a way that makes me feel good about myself. I have learned to no longer sacrifice my mental health in regard to living up to a fake ideal body image. I refuse to accept images of women thrown in my face all day that do not celebrate the vast array of women's bodies. I celebrate my inner wild and call bullshit on the nonexistent woman every time I see her.

Taking Back Our Bodies

Now that we know the way social and mass media uses images of the nonexistent woman to control our inner wild, we have the power to take back our bodies. We start taking back our bodies from social and mass media not only by rejecting fake images of women, but by displaying ourselves in social and mass media on our own terms. Thankfully we now celebrate curves more in today's world than a few decades ago, but we still have a long way to go. We have no control over how the powers that be display women, but we do have power and control over how we choose to display ourselves.

The bottom line is the focus needs to shift from us as how we "should look" as women to the negative behavior aimed at stealing our inner wild. Rather than judge a woman for posting an image of her celebrating feeling sexy, celebrate her. Encourage her to embrace her body and sexuality full force. Instead of telling me to dress more modestly, let's focus on your lack of basic control, human decency, and respect in how you treat women. Regardless of how we choose to display ourselves as women on our own social media, we are fully and rightfully allowed to take full ownership of how we choose to show our bodies and sexuality.

How we choose to own and even display our bodies as women is up to us, and us alone. I have powerful female friends who show gorgeous, sexy pictures of themselves on their social media. They take full ownership of their inner wild. It only becomes demeaning when dominating comments are made by men who aim to take away our power to display our bodies and sexuality on our own terms, and only then do we hand them our power if we let them have it. We have the absolute power to delete their comments. We can choose to address their comments head on and expose their sad attempts to demean us as women. We can assertively point out we appreciate being admired for our beauty and prefer not to be mentally undressed. It simply does not matter what our armchair critics have to say regarding our bodies and sexuality.

As a graduate student, I dedicated my entire dissertation, The Self as Text: A Qualitative Examination of Mass Media Influence on Adult Female Television Series Fans' Sexual Identity, on the ways social and mass media influence women's body image and sexuality. I finished my dissertation in 2009, yet these words remain openly valid today. I look forward to the day my words become outdated:

Where do women go from present feminism? If they dress up and show off their feminine sexuality are they mere patriarchal objects or owning and celebrating subjectification/ownership of their sexuality? It appears today's feminist movement has become dichotomous and confusing to say the least – women are damned if they wear stilettos with lipstick and damned if they don't. As the discussion on the current state of divided feminism draws to a close, I can only hope there is some type of compromise that can be reached for women in society.

It's never too late to fall in love with your body. I don't know about you, but I love feeling and looking sexy. I love taking photos of myself where I celebrate my body and sexuality. It feels good to feel good. I know that when I post these pictures of myself, I will have my fair share of critics. When I see a friend post a picture of herself where she is feeling FINE, I always try to boost her up! We can take our bodies back together by moving forward in taking ownership of our body image in social and mass media to support other women who choose to feel sexy in their bodies. Let's fix each other's crowns. When women show they are feeling beautiful on their own terms, let's celebrate each other! Let's empower one another through our re-wilding journeys as we assume power over our bodies and sexuality once and for all in society.

I would like to add, there is nothing wrong with doing things to our appearance that make us feel better about ourselves! If you don't feel comfortable in your body, it can be incredibly empowering to lose or gain weight. Aesthetically altering our appearance can only be harmful to our self-esteem when we do it to gain the love or approval of others. Altering your appearance for yourself can be a powerful act of self-love. I have had dear friends undergo bariatric and other types of plastic surgery who are living their best lives. If you don't like something about yourself, it is ok to change it on your own terms.

I don't want to sound like a hypocrite here so I will share that when my daughter was four years old, I got breast implants. I tried my best to live with the fact that my former, full breasts had shrunk to smaller than an A cup after nursing my daughter. I was a negative size A, not kidding. I wore a size A water bra every day to compensate for the fact my breasts had magically disappeared. The fact is I had no breasts and as a woman who loves her natural curves, I missed having curves on top of my body too. For four years I tried to convince myself as a strong, independent woman

I didn't want breasts. I finally decided I wanted breasts again and for myself, not for anyone else. My only regret is not getting them sooner.

Our bodies are as unique as our fingerprints. We have every right to outright reject images of women we see in social and mass media we know are unrealistic. We can teach our sons and daughters to do the same. We deserve the right to treat our bodies with love and respect. As women, far too often we see our body as defining us rather than embracing the precious body we are in. Baby, you were born wild. Choose to re-wild by rejecting the nonexistent woman and love the body you are in.

Mindful Action

So where do we go from here to empower ourselves as women? Even if we tried to cut out all social and mass media from our lives it is all but impossible. As women, we have every right to enjoy the benefits of social and mass media. Engaging in social and mass media has become a primary source of pleasure and escape from everyday life into an exciting, vibrant netherworld. It takes little effort to enjoy mass media. We can also use social and mass media for re-wilding inspiration. Choose empowering and women positive algorithms when you can. Post your inner wild. If a sexy selfie makes you feel good, own it!

Keeping a critical eye open allows us the space we need to celebrate our bodies and sexuality on our own terms. We have the power to reject negative behavior aimed to train and suppress us as women as "normal". It's not normal to have our inner wild suppressed. It makes us feel like shit and affects everything in our life from our sense of self-worth to the quality of our intimate relationships.

For far too long our armchair critics who feel their masculinity is boosted by turning us into sexual objects have thrived because we have been caught in the "damned if I do and damned if I don't look sexy today" trap. It is long overdue that the focus is removed from us as women and placed on their negative behavior. We have every right to reject their opinion. We must also teach our young men and women to recognize the ways powerful forces in our culture and society train us, often subconsciously, to objectify women's bodies and sexuality. We must teach our future leaders to do better.

When it comes to your body image, the ultimate act of re-wilding is to love your unique, one-of-a-kind body exactly as it is. We deserve to celebrate and embrace our bodies. In addition, supporting our fellow sisters goes a long way! Let's learn to continue to support one another and remove ourselves as critics of each other. There is plenty of room in this world for every woman to celebrate herself. We can start a worldwide sisterhood of acceptance and support for one another where we feel safe to express our bodies on our own terms.

Now that we have explored re-wilding your body image in healthy, positive ways we are entering the final stage of our body image journey together. Learning to love your body takes time. Be kind to yourself. Start re-wilding by practicing self-love every day.

Self-Reflection Exercise: The Unbecoming

You will need your re-wilding journal for this self-reflection exercise. Please write your thoughts to the following questions: Write down at least 10 things you like about your body. Reflect on this list as often as you need to.

What, if any, are your negative body image triggers? For example, do you feel comfortable having sex with the lights on or going to the swimming pool or beach? Take a moment to self-reflect and write about what impact this has on your actual life. Your re-wilding action item moving forward is to keep a sharp, critical eye on the ways women are displayed in social and mass media. Notice when an image or negative headline of a woman makes you feel uncomfortable. Sit with this feeling for a moment. Analyze why this particular piece of social or mass media negatively affects you. Tune into your inner wild and take back your power. Refer to your list of the top 10 things you love about your body.

Now that you have learned how to re-wild your assets by taking back your body, the next step of your re-wilding journey is to (re)connect and awaken your sexual wild side. Research suggests that the more comfortable we are with our bodies, the more likely it is we will experience greater positive sexual satisfaction in our life. In the following chapter we are going to explore our divine femininity through connecting with our sexuality in healthy, positive ways. Be prepared for a wild sexual awakening!

Chapter 9: Re-Wilding Your Sexuality

"No woman gets an orgasm from shining a kitchen floor." - Betty Friedan

"The vagina is the most powerful weapon in the universe." I nearly choked on my coffee as I heard my teenage daughter tell her friend this the other day at our house. I was proud to hear her say this. Maybe my teenage daughter does listen to me! I have mentioned the vagina as the most powerful weapon in the universe to her on multiple occasions half-jokingly, but I mean every word when I say it.

There is tremendous power in being a sexual woman. If we ever doubt it all we need to do is reflect upon the ways our sexuality has been the target of systematic oppression by cultural and societal forces since the dawn of time and recorded history. Across planet earth there has been a consistent, global trend of trying to control women in nearly every culture and society in existence and this trend still continues today. This mass un-wilding primarily begins with socialization control tactics aimed at directly suppressing our bodies and sexuality to assert male ownership of and suppress, tame and control, you guessed it, your most powerful weapon.

I am so happy you have made it to this point in the book! Our journey to reconnect with our inner wild would not be complete without openly exploring all the fun parts of our sexuality. My goal in talking about sex is to help you feel empowered to begin your own sexual revolution according to your own unique desires and values.

Ladies, it's time to explore your sexual wild side! Let's begin.

Putting the "Ohhhhh" Back in Your Orgasm

"Orgasms are one of the healthiest forms of stress release. So, when I tell you to go fuck yourself it's because I care." - **Unknown**

Let's talk about sex. Wet. Wild. Sweaty. Dripping, electric, erotic, eyes rolling in the back of your head, moaning, ecstatic sex.

Our bodies are precious. Our bodies are incredibly powerful. We are blessed with the ability to grow precious life and give birth. We are blessed with the ability to adopt and nurture children like they are our own. Women are unique in the fact that having an orgasm is something we have evolved to enjoy! Re-wilding your sexuality is one of the best acts of self-love you can do for yourself and is a beautiful gift to share with someone you love. Re-wilding our sexuality helps bring us not only closer to ourselves but can create electrifying bonds of intimacy and pleasure with our partner. When we re-wild our sexuality we allow ourselves to experience pleasure on an entirely new level. Being wild in bed is a LOT of fun!

As women we are taught to put others' needs ahead of our own. As a result, we put ourselves last in the bedroom too. Assuming ownership of our sexuality as women is a huge deal. Taking back our sexuality is a rebellious act of re-wilding that allows you to feel all the pleasure you should feel in bed (or in an elevator, the woods, in the backseat of your car outside a PTA meeting, stairwell, on your desk at work, etc.). Orgasms are not a privilege. They are your right. Our loving partners deeply want to see us enjoy our right to orgasm as often and intensely as possible. Yet recent research shows less than 46% of young and middle-aged adult women express (1) they are not feeling sexually satisfied, (2) are not discussing it with their partners, and (3) as a result experience a drop in happiness in their intimate relationships.

Women are far less likely to have an orgasm during sex than

men. Only 6% of women report having regular orgasms during sex, whereas men experience an orgasm 96% of the time. Fact: we have a huge orgasm gap with our male lovers. It's not even a gap, it's the Grand Canyon. Here's the bottom line. It doesn't need to be this way. We can have the same rate of orgasms as men experience and more. If you are lesbian, you are likely climaxing more than a heterosexual woman is. Research shows lesbian women climax 13% more often than heterosexual women. The lesbian effect is real. Carry on! If you are heterosexual, this next section is for you.

The Pleasure War

Humans are the only primates on the planet that can engage in sex for pleasure and not just solely for reproductive reasons. Do you know we have over 8,000 nerve endings in the clitoris alone? Not only that, but the clitoris is also the only human organ that exists solely to produce sexual pleasure for women. And here is a newsflash, **96% of men have orgasms during intercourse** due to the fact their nerve endings are supercharged in the tip of their penis. Since intercourse often does not include clitoral stimulation, which is where the vast majority of women's orgasm-inducing nerves reside, well, you can see why men have orgasms from intercourse 1,500% more often than we do. You read that correctly. Men are capable of having 1,500% more orgasms than women during intercourse.

It's time to put our pleasure first. Our lovers seek to prioritize our needs, so we should too. Let's be honest. We all fake orgasms from time to time. We would never admit this to our lover. We see how hard they work to please us. When you are close to orgasming and saying, "I'm so close! Don't stop!" but they move their finger or tongue just one millimeter to the left - you lose it - but fake that shit anyway to avoid making it awkward. Your lover is going above and beyond to rub your hotspot but is missing it entirely. You say nothing and fake that shit anyway.

Your partner is taking you from behind and it feels better than nothing, but you get zero clitoral stimulation so there is no way you are going to climax. Your partner is completely oblivious to the fact your clitoris is left out of the equation. Rather than fake it, you take charge and jump on top so you can take control of your clitoral stimulation. You are SO close then your lover grabs your hips and starts pumping you up and down like a fucking jackhammer. You instantly lose it and you guessed it; you fake that shit anyway just to get it to stop.

Let's face it, if you like men, whether you like it or not chances are your man has watched porn. Research indicates over 98% of men have watched porn in the past six months, compared to 73% of women. Yes, we watch porn too. You know who you are and I am right there with you. Not all porn is vile. There is a lot of porn that is highly educational and sensual. Porn is the one industry where women get paid twice as much as men. One of my close friends is a former porn star. I have immense respect for sex workers who take charge of their sexual essence and capitalize off it. But here's my point. Women in porn are paid to be a fantasy. Men are the main consumers of porn so as the target audience for the industry women are shown in positions that please men. Rarely is porn about pleasing a woman's clitoris. In fact, it is often neglected to get the main pound town money shots.

After years of consuming porn and us faking orgasms, it is no wonder men may think the way to get us off is to fuck us like a jackrabbit in a porn film. Until we tell our male lovers what we need, there is no way we can expect them to know how to help us climax. Putting your clitoris first means it can get awkward. You need to tell your lover when they slip one millimeter to the left and you lose it. You can take care of yourself while your lover takes you from behind. If you have not done that before, trust me, it might be your new favorite position! Get on top and do your thing and let your partner lay there and enjoy the view. Most importantly, don't fake an orgasm to get the sex to stop.

If you are not enjoying the moment, switch it up so you both can. Buy a selection of delicious vibrators so you can enjoy it when your partner wants to go to pound town. Old school vibrators that look like a massive penis are a thing of the past. Most vibrators are now beautifully engineered with your clitoral pleasure in mind and look more like a spaceship, so your man won't be threatened by using a toy. Keep a copy of the Kama Sutra in your bedside table and your fun toys charged up and ready to go!

Take the time you need to orgasm. Our partner deserves to experience our honest pleasure, even if it makes it awkward because it takes longer. Pleasing you makes your lover feel incredibly fulfilled. And ladies, I think it goes without saying if your lover doesn't want to prioritize your clitoris, you need to find a new one. Cheap lovers are also cheap outside of the bedroom. Put your pleasure first and remember, don't fake it till you make it.

Leave Her Wild

Being raised Mormon religion I learned very quickly from a young age how young girls were expected to behave. I remember significant moments when I felt my inner wild being domesticated. At church on Sundays, I was expected to wear a dress. Even today, Mormon women are expected to wear dresses to church. Regardless of the fact there may be three feet of snow on the ground, and it was below zero winter temperatures, females are frowned upon if they wear pants to a Mormon Sunday church service.

Before I could even read, I wondered why I had to walk through snow and on ice in winters in a dress with little, shiny dress shoes on while the boys got to wear long pants and warm shoes that covered their feet. My legs were icicles, and my feet were often freezing and soaking wet after tiptoeing through the wintry slush in the church parking lot. Once inside the church, I had to sit like a lady as I thawed out. During breaks between our three-hour church service girls did not run around as openly as the boys. It was as if we knew we had to behave differently before we tiptoed through the snow in the parking lot. The very clothing I was expected to wear because I was not a boy was my first realization as a child of the distinct division of gender roles and expectations placed on girls versus boys.

As a young pre-pubescent girl, I was taught as a female my role was to grow up a virgin and to marry one man and be with this one man for all time and eternity. Mormons take being married for all time and eternity seriously. They have a separate institution of marriage outside of our legal system that keeps you married to your husband long after you die. Absolutely no gay marriage is allowed in the Mormon church, one of the many oppressive reasons I reject the religion.

In and outside of the Mormon church, as the world began to teach me who I "should" be, I learned to try to win the approval of others. As many of us do, I did what I was supposed to do because it made others happy. In Dr. Pavlov's historical psychology experiment, all he had to do was ring a bell to train dogs to salivate for a treat. Similarly, society quickly teaches us from a young age how we need to behave to be accepted or rejected. I was trained to silence my inner wild and perform the appropriate response to society's expectant stimulus. Our behavior according to what we "should" do ultimately puts us in the position of being included in our communities or suffering the consequence of being a lonely outcast. Being included means we feel more loved, being rejected means the opposite. I wanted to be included and loved, so I allowed myself to be trained into a well-behaved girl. I acted like a good girl to get a treat and a pat on the head.

As I grew up going to church, I attended "homemaking" meetings for women only, of course, while the men were learning how to be patriarchal "leaders." The boys were being taught to "be" somebody while we girls were being taught to "find" somebody. The stark contrast of the male versus female roles in the Mormon church was indelibly imprinted on my mind. Girls are not allowed to serve sacrament. Women are not allowed to serve in decision-making leadership roles. All the Mormon church prophets are male as well as his 12 apostles. I felt completely stifled and bored and restless and confused and frustrated. I felt my inner wild being choked out by the ruffled dresses I was wearing, and the patriarchal bullshit being spouted from the pulpit.
I tried so hard to believe in what I was taught in the Mormon church. I wanted so much to find the same solace in the Mormon church my friends and relatives seemed to (and still do today). As hard as I naively prayed to believe in Mormonism, I could not find a sense of security and comfort in the religion. I felt my spirituality alive inside of me. I was spiritual, not religious. As I struggled

to fit in at church I failed miserably. I was too wild to be Mormon.

The final moment for me involved a meeting with my church ward leader, or Bishop. I was nineteen. I explained the "major" sins I committed and confessed "I feel guilty because I don't feel guilty." My mom had taught me that "sex is natural" so I did not understand why I should feel shame and guilt over enjoying my sexuality. It was at this moment I came to realize the Mormon cocktail of sexual guilt and overt control of my divine sexual essence was unacceptable to me.

I explained to my Bishop how the "sins of the flesh" I enjoyed engaging in, a.k.a. lustful premarital sex, were completely natural and stated plainly I felt no shame whatsoever for the choices I make with my body. This was the moment I knew my inner wild had won. I had my own approval and no longer sought the approval nor social acceptance of a religion I did not believe in. I left the Mormon church and never looked back.

Obviously being Mormon was not a good fit for me, but it is for many of my dear friends and family. I respect their choice and I appreciate the love they still have for me even as I became an "apostate". An apostate is a strong word in the Mormon faith. It is the term used when someone no longer chooses to remain active in the church or when the church refuses to let them be a part of the religion. As apostates we are seen as projects. The church takes pity on us. Many feel it is impossible to be happy, well-adjusted humans if we are not active Mormons. We are also going to hell. The Mormon missionaries still find me from time to time and I am always very kind to them and respect the sacrifice they are making for their values and beliefs. I also tell them I'd rather be a ruler in hell than a follower in heaven and they are wasting their time on me.

Regardless of my rejection of the Mormon church, part of re-wilding is appreciating where we end up while also celebrating others along their own personal journeys. We all love, support and value one another exactly as we are, and that feels good. I'm grateful for my Mormon experience because I exited the religion with a strong spiritual relationship with my higher power fully intact. I love the quote by Laurel Thatcher Ulrich "Well behaved women seldom make history," to which I'd like to add, "May all women embrace their inner wild and live life on their own terms with heart and soul." Leave us wild. Let us howl at the moon.

Re-Wilding Your Sexual Revolution

Not long after high school, I moved to Manhattan, New York. The largest city I had been to prior to moving to New York was Salt Lake City, Utah. I enrolled in the Fashion Institute of Technology (F.I.T.) and lived in Chelsea. New York City blew me away. There was opportunity everywhere! It was everything I had seen on television and more. I was young and finally free of the restrictions of living in a small town where everyone knew one another, had all likely dated each other already, and there was an extreme lack of privacy. I was on a re-wilding mission to see the world and be free.

New York also chewed me up and spit me out. I was a little country mouse. I remember showing up at F.I.T. in a cowboy hat and boots. I was laughed at. I had zero street smarts and I was mugged my first week there, but I learned fast. One of the first things I did was head to Times Square to get a fake I.D. I ditched the cowboy boots for heels and my wardrobe quickly adjusted to fit in as well. I may have been raised in Wyoming, but I definitely grew up in New York City.

Within a few weeks of moving to New York, I met a man from the Bronx. He had me at hello with his charisma and thick Bronx born and raised accent. He gave me butterflies. One night, after being intimate, we had a candid conversation that would change my life. He asked me if I had an orgasm. I told him yes. What we did felt good so thought I had. I had been having sex for years, but I had no idea what an orgasm was. He then kindly explained to me he could not be intimate with me again until I was comfortable in my own body. He encouraged me to learn to have an orgasm and then call him. I asked him how I could have an orgasm without him giving me one. It was then that I learned I cannot expect my partner to please me if I don't know how to please myself.

I had never masturbated until I moved to Manhattan because I was taught it was a sin. The few times I thought about it I felt like God and my grandparents, and even your grandparents, were watching. So, one night I put on some Enigma, lit some candles and I had my first orgasm. I was 20 years old. I had my first mind blowing orgasm that night. Afterwards, I cried. I cried with relief because it was as if all of my years of natural sexual frustration had just erupted right then and there. I cried because I had neglected to truly get to know my own body for so long. I cried with happiness knowing my life would never be the same. Thank you gorgeous man from the Bronx for refusing to be with me again until I loved myself first!

When I moved to the Big Apple, I could be whoever the hell I wanted to be and I let all of me re-wild like a lion let loose from a cage. My first year in Manhattan was delicious and decadent. I indulged in safe and trusting sexual acts, intimacy and fantasies that truly let my personal inner wild roam free. I had never been surrounded by so many beautiful men of all shapes, sizes, and accents. After going out dancing until 4 AM I spent the rest of a weekend with an Italian Stallion named Vincente Spitola. Re-wilding over an entire weekend became a decadent hobby for me. I spent weekends on a whim with some of the most beautiful, sensual men I had ever laid eyes on from all corners of New Jersey and the world. I relished in BDSM. I bought nipple clamps, crotchless panties and lacy thigh high stockings. I kept the Kama Sutra by my bedside. As I re-wilded my sexuality according to my personal value system, I began a love affair with my own body.

It was during my sexual revolution for the first time in my young life, I began to absolutely love and celebrate the body I was in. I felt a positive change in my life spiritually, psychologically, and physically. As I embraced my sexuality, I embraced my whole self. I was free of any shame I was taught I should feel when I celebrated my sexuality. Sexual shame was and is no longer a problem for me. I will profess it is incredibly liberating to readily reject sexual shame. Sexual shame has no place in my life and that is because I embrace and celebrate my sexuality on my own terms. When it comes to my sexuality, I am wild and free and it feels sensational.

Having an orgasm is your God given right. It is one of the most joyful, natural experiences you can have. One of the most important things to remember here is we cannot expect our partner to please us if we do not know how to please ourselves. Our sexual re-wilding starts with self-awareness and self-love. Whatever that may look like for you, I encourage you to love yourself right where you are at and embrace your body's natural intimate desires.

Re-Wilding the Infamous Double Standard

When we celebrate our sexual essence, we are celebrating our inner wild. Embracing our sexuality not only taps right into releasing our inner wild, it helps improve our physical, spiritual and psychological health. But when it comes to re-wilding our sexual side, it can be far easier said than done. For us as women, our sexual identities are not only physical, but they are also deeply psychological and spiritual.

Since the dawn of recorded history, our sexuality has been compartmentalized and spoon fed to us in extremes by the powers that be in society. Either we are "wife" and maternal "mom" material, or we have too much sexual desire and that makes us a "whore." We are usually put in either the "Madonna or the Whore" stereotype. The sexual stigmas that we encounter in regard to our sexuality can prevent us from embracing our own unique sexual essence and needs. As women our sexuality is constantly judged and yes, even shamed. To re-wild it is long overdue we as women refuse to feel shame when it comes to sex.

Try as we may in our modern world, we still suffer from the double standard of males being allowed to be freer with their sexuality than women. Lucky guys! Case in point, men are still not referred to as promiscuous in a derogatory manner. They are still considered sexy and virile the more women they can get and the more sex they have. It is shocking that even in today's world my daughter even hears the words "slut" and "whore" being tossed around at her high school by kids to describe girls, not the boys, in a hateful way. And let's be clear here, it's not just the boys who slut shame the girls. The girls call other girls sluts and whores as well.

As parents and older family members to our future generation of young women and men it is imperative we remain aware of these hegemonic stereotypes and model positive, inclusive, respectful behavior for our children to understand women are not objects to be controlled mentally, physically, or sexually. Whether we realize it or not, it is still deeply ingrained in us to continue to teach our boys, and yes, our girls too, to perpetuate the double standard of women as weak and men as strong. The fact is our children are learning this from someone. I hope it's not the parents but after working in education for 20 years I can meet a student and I know exactly how they are raised by their parents within 15 minutes of interacting with them.

Let's start by teaching our little boys not to feel shame when they feel emotion. It's ok for them to feel emotion and not to be pressured to "man-up." We need to teach our children using terms that are feminine as insults to demean others are not ok. When we tell little boys to "stop crying like a girl" we teach them girls are weak. The same goes for calling someone a "pussy" or "drama queen." Why do we have "working mothers" but not working fathers? I could go on and on about ways our everyday language berates females. Betty White had a great point when she said "Why do people say, 'Grow some balls?' Balls are weak and sensitive. If you really wanna get tough, grow a vagina. Those things really take a pounding!" Preach it, Betty!

Own Your Inner Whore

It is long overdue we put the Madonna-Whore stereotype and social control of women inbed. Our right to experience sexual pleasure has long been controlled by social forces within our educational system, religions, popular culture, images of women in mass media and family attitudes. Throughout history societal authorities have feared female sexual desires would become uncontrollable if we were allowed to indulge in our sexuality for pleasure.

Allowing women to be sexually free terrifies traditionalists, also referred to as those (female and male) who benefit from controlling our sexuality. Women embracing their sexuality endangers the traditional sanctity of marriage and the entire social order in general. If we all wildly indulge in our sexual desires it could begin the end of the traditional, domesticating, controlling world as we know it and that's a good thing! Just imagine a world where we are no longer feared nor villainized for being the "whore" rather than the "Madonna" for a moment. It is long overdue we end the mass un-wilding of our most powerful weapon by celebrating our sexuality on our own terms.

I have a concert t-shirt with a picture of the gorgeous Barbie look-a-like rockstar and lead singer of In This Moment, Maria Brink, on the front wearing a dunce cap with the word "Whore" painted on it in bright red letters. She wrote a song called Whore and when she introduces this song live, in concert she absolutely explains taking ownership of this word back for all women. Although Maria may look like the ultimate vision of what society would set as the standard of a perfect blonde Barbie doll, make no mistake about it, she is a strong, bad ass woman taking back ownership of the word Whore in a powerful way. It is long overdue that we take complete ownership of our sexuality on our own terms according to our own personal value systems.

Re-Wilding on Your Terms

Whatever your belief system, I hope you can carve out the sacred space you deserve to celebrate your female sexuality in a way that empowers you to not only love the body you are in but to experience strong self-love and intimacy throughout your life. Part of re-wilding is allowing yourself to embrace and enjoy your sexual, sensual self. As women growing up in society, we often feel a lot of emotion, and even shame, when our sexuality is brought up. This goes against our innate wild nature as women. We are born hardwired for pleasurable sex and there is no shame in that. As women, we were born to be wet and wild.

When it comes to sex are you holding back? Are you faking it? If so, you are not alone. Many women are on a journey to embrace their sexuality. Take a moment to get in touch with your body in a way that makes you feel amazing. I urge you to make a sexual wellness goal for yourself and go for it! Reflect on it in your re-wilding journal. Take time to re-wild your sexuality every day. Read and reflect the following affirmations as many times as you need to and please feel free to edit away and make them as naughty as you need them to be. Enjoy.

- I deserve to feel sexy and sexual.
- I trust my body fully.
- I deserve to feel intense sexual pleasure with myself and with my lover.
- My body and mind are one and in harmony.
- My body knows what to do.
- I am re-wilding my sexuality on my own terms.
- I release all thoughts that do not serve me.

In the next chapter, I have a surprise for you. Did you know everything you hope and dream for in life can literally be delivered to you if you trust in your inner wild? We are going to explore how your inner wild is in tune with the universe, and they can work together to deliver your greatest dreams to you.

Chapter 10: Your Inner Wild at Work

"What you think, you become. What you feel, you attract. What you imagine, you create." **Buddha**

One of the most life-changing and exhilarating projects I have worked on during my consulting career so far has been the inaugural Inner MBA with Sounds True Publishing, LinkedIn, Wisdom 2.0 and MindfulNYU. The Inner MBA program is a culmination of these prestigious organizations coming together to create an innovative, forward-thinking leadership program for current and future leaders on a mission to meet the demands of today's ever-changing leadership. The Inner MBA dives far deeper than a traditional MBA program by creating forward-thinking, innovative leaders from the inside out.

As much as we bash the millennials, we have them to thank for refusing to put up with traditional workplace bullshit we grew up with. We know old forms of top down, patriarchal leadership at work are quickly becoming outdated and no longer work. We now know we deserve to be treated with inclusive compassion in the workplace that allows us to have more flexible schedules. If we are unhappy with our jobs, we can simply apply for a new one with the click of our mouse. Companies know they need to do better to attract and keep talent. The program is highly innovative and teaches emotional intelligence and mindful meditation practices that allow leaders to take an eco-friendly, emotionally intelligent, inclusive, compassionate leadership approach for greater success. Throughout the duration of this project, I had the opportunity to work with over 30-plus successful leaders in their fields ranging from academic scholars to internationally influential CEOs whose work contributes to making the world a better place. I noticed a common trait on how they got started that related to their bottom-line advice on how to achieve your life's goals and that was to "Trust the universe will give you what you want." Along their journey, many of these CEO's risked losing their secure day jobs and chose to leave a safe, secure job to pursue their dream.

Each of these successful people overcame their fear of a steady paycheck from a job that didn't feed their soul to be true to their dreams. They embraced their inner wild and knew the universe would deliver. The only difference I found between them and "us" is they went for their dreams and trusted their intuition, the voice of their inner wild, that their risk would pay off. It worked for them, and it can work for you too. We are going to go deep in this chapter. We are going to challenge the un-wilding beliefs we have grown up to believe keep us safe, because they are causing mass misery. You are now ready to put your inner wild to work for you to experience success on your own terms. We begin by examining why we as women need to reimagine the American Dream. In its current state, the American Dream is a hoax aimed to control your inner wild and prevents us from pursuing meaningful work.

Ditching the American Dream

The American Dream is a lie. Not only is it killing our inner wild, but it is also killing us in the process of pursuing it. It is time for women to reimagine the American dream and how it needs to work for us on our own terms. Our inner wild is most often our greatest passion in life that we have been trained, even rewarded, not to use because we are taught to follow a specific path in life. We are conditioned from a young age in order to be successful and happy we should (1) be potty trained (2) graduate from high school, (3) graduate from college, (4) get a job, (5) get married, (6) buy a house with a picket fence we only occupy weeknights and weekends (7) raise a family, and (8) do this until we retire at the age of 65 when our lives are past the point of being halfway over. Before we know it, our life has flown by and we spent more than half of our adult life in a job that we can't wait to retire from. When we retire, we have one foot in the grave as far as the years we have left in life. Living the American Dream steals the best years of our life. It's a rip-off.

The American Dream is meant to give us hope. It is meant to inspire us to rise from the depths of poverty to become anything from a future president to an astronaut. The concept of the American Dream is a problem because it is so far out of reach for most of us. Research shows social mobility in America is the lowest of all developed countries. That means if you are born poor in the United States, you are more likely to stay that way here than in any other Westernized country. The U.S. is far from embodying the land of opportunity. We are taught that if we work hard enough, we can achieve anything. Yet most of us are overworked and still struggle to keep up with skyrocketing costs of living and housing. Unlike us 99%ers, the majority of current millionaires inherited their wealth. The greatest fallacy of the American Dream is that we are taught it is our fault if we don't reach our dreams, not the system that fails us.

Most of us are more than familiar with what it feels like to work in a job we hate, but we may not realize it can be a death sentence. Sitting and atrophying in a cubicle day after day is not what we expected the American Dream to be. It goes against our inner wild to clock in and clock out to work in a row of cubicles under fluorescent lights for 40-plus hours per week for 45-plus years or longer. Ever notice how we all have meetings about meetings and how it slowly kills you inside? It is unhealthy for us to wake up each weekday and perform like ants in an anthill. Have you ever stopped to notice people's faces when they are commuting to work in traffic either in their cars or on the bus or subway? We all look tired and unhappy as if our life is slowly being drained out of us day by day. When we allow our inner wild to be tamed it can make us miserable not just as women, but as a human race.

It goes against our very nature as human beings to sit in cubicles and traffic. From Los Angeles, Mumbai, to Houston, there is not one human on the face of this planet who looks forward to sitting in traffic. In addition to spending hours adding up to years of our lives in traffic, we spend more time with our coworkers than we do with our own families. We sacrifice time with our loved ones, precious time that makes our hearts happy, for the fallacy of the American Dream.

The single greatest factor attributed to stress in life is, drum roll please, our jobs. The chaos of adulting is amplified for us as women. We are often balancing multiple roles in life ranging from marriages, relationships, work, family, fur babies and more. Some days it feels like the best we can do is just get through the day in one piece. As women, we are often taking care of others and sacrificing ourselves, which can often leave us depleted. Stanford professor, Jeffrey Pfeffer, states American work environments are the fifth leading cause of deaths in the country each year. We work long hours. We have chaotic schedules. We fear being laid off. For those of us who get laid off, there is a 44% chance we will commit suicide or die from alcohol misuse in four years if we don't find a job.

We have all worked for that toxic boss that has taken years from our lives. We have to struggle to find any sense of work-life balance. Exercise is a luxury to fit into our schedules before we tire from our workday. We have demanding jobs with low pay. The cost of living is going up at a far faster rate than our salaries. Unfavorable work environments defy our natural inner wild, yet we continue to accept these circumstances and tell ourselves "Oh well. Such is life." We go to bed exhausted only to wake up and do it all again the next morning.

We know the one-size-fits-all white picket fences fallacy of "livin' the American Dream" makes us miserable to the point of death, yet we are stuck in the rut of believing this is all life has to offer. Many of us follow the formula of the American Dream. We graduated from high school. Some of us went to college. We work hard to pay off our lifelong debt. We overwork ourselves. We do what we are supposed to do and more, so why are we so damn unhappy? The answer is simple. We are sick and tired because not only are we doing too much, we do far too little of what sparks a fire inside of our inner wild soul. You can trust your inner wild is exactly what you need to tap into to live your best life. Your inner wild can help you manifest your truest desire to live and work on our own terms resulting in a more fulfilled life. Eleanor Roosevelt said, "The future belongs to those who believe in the beauty of their dreams." You deserve to make your dreams come true.

Empty Houses

Recently I met a woman who decided to pack up and move from Denver to Montana and live her dream of opening a yoga and meditation center. She had worked at a community college for the majority of her career. She had a stable state job and a reliable pension. It was during the Covid-19 pandemic when she and her husband had a chance to actually enjoy the home they left every day to work so hard to pay for. She told me, "Every day I would drive by these empty houses and wonder why we are in debt for over half of our lives for a house we only sleep in, like a hotel?" She and her husband and two children moved to Montana, she launched her successful business, and she has not looked back. The last time I spoke with her she said they absolutely love it.

Speaking of empty houses, most of us know what it is like to work to an extent you feel like the home you are working so hard to pay for is more of a hotel and a place of recovery on the weekends after an exhausting week. I was there for many years. I was so grateful to have a decent career that allowed me to provide for my child. I almost felt guilty for wanting more. Almost. I felt as if I had sold my soul just to make a decent living. I found out quickly I was living at work and overworking myself to pay for an empty house.

I used to commute from a suburb in Denver to my job downtown. For a year I took an express bus and each morning I would get to the parking lot as early as I could after dropping my daughter off in the long parent line at her school. I don't know if you have experienced this but parents in the long drop off lines at kids' schools are often stressed and grumpy. Never mess with a mom in a minivan. She is on a serious mission to get her kids where they need to go. I have mad respect for busy moms, and I get the hell out of their way in the school drop off lines.

Taking the express bus is faster than driving and being

stuck in Denver traffic. The winters in Denver can be brutal and when it snows traffic comes to a standstill. Denver becomes a slippery parking lot. The buses are often late due to the snow. There were many days I would wait outside for the express bus in work clothes and subzero temperatures in the blowing snow, standing in a line slowly shuffling towards the bus entrance hoping there would be a seat available. I stood on the bus for the 45-minute commute as it got more and more crowded, and no seats were available. We were packed in together like a bunch of little unhappy sardines.

I watched the same guy pick his nose and ass on the Denver commuter express bus for two fucking years. After he dug deep, he would go back to holding the bus pole with his fingers. It literally made me gag. I will never touch bus or subway poles again without my shirt over my hand for the rest of my life. The booger and ass picker was actually cute and wore a wedding ring. Someone got to live with that every day. Yay. I was living my best life as an ant. Commuting on the express bus to downtown Denver was another version of hell. It was also $8 a day. Hardly a bargain. Driving was cheaper. I ditched the misery of the commuter bus and began driving to work. I sold my empty house and moved to a high rise across the street from my job and Chloe's school. I was no longer a slave to my empty house payment. I gained three hours of my life back each day.

I love the movie Office Space and the TV show The Office (both the British and US versions). They are funny because they allow us to laugh at the 40-hour per week work existence, because, well, it sucks! Re-wilding gives you the power to capitalize on what makes you thrive.

Burn the Box

When we return to our inner wild it is much harder to put us in a box. There are many boxes that society uses to define us. It is easy to put people, especially women, in boxes. Our brains are hardwired to categorize people to understand each other better. We are often defined by our outward selves, the side of us we present to the world. Rarely are we defined by our inner wild, our true selves. We have been conditioned our entire lives to get to know others by the roles they have in society, and thus the box they are in, but being confined to a box can also be like living in a prison without bars. The problem with boxes is it is impossible to take each unique person and define them by a box. When we are put into a box, we are a part of the rank-and-file system. Regardless of whether it is a positive or negative box, when we are put into a box, we are judged, filed, ranked, and labeled. We are far more than our box. It is time to take your box, set it on fire and watch it burn.

My only regret in life would be to die with regrets. When I turned 40, I realized my life was close to halfway over. I still felt young, but I fully realized my time on this planet was tick-tocking away. I say this half-jokingly but if I was lucky enough to live to 80 years old, then yes, technically I felt I had one foot in my grave. Realizing my own mortality in this way sets me free to burn boxes used to define me. I felt like I needed to make better use of my time on this earth. To that point in my life, I felt I had "behaved." I had done everything I was "supposed to do". Now, I was going to do whatever I wanted to do! Some may call this a midlife crisis. I prefer to call this a midlife awakening.

I really tried hard to fit into the good girl box. I wasted years trying to force my inner wild into silence to fit into what I thought my peers at work and in life expected from me. I felt my natural resistance to being domesticated was something I needed to hide to gain the approval of others. I spent years trying to ignore and smother my true nature. As much as we may try and ignore her, our inner wild is a fire that refuses to be put out. I ultimately failed at putting myself in a traditional, good girl box.

My failure to suppress my inner wild has been my greatest success. One of the biggest mistakes I made in my life and career was assuming my resistance to being domesticated into the female roles society assigned to me meant there may be something wrong with me. For years I tried to suppress my inner wild to feel more accepted as a wild woman in a boxed in world. I could never comprehend why I never wanted (and still don't) a traditional life or marriage that did not fit in a box that people could understand. Growing up I remember all my girlfriends excitedly talking about their dream wedding. I had zero interest in getting married. Ever. I have always seen picket fences as prison bars. Thus far, I am too much of a free-spirited gypsy to live a traditional life with a husband and 1.2 children.

The boxes in society formulate our identity in a multitude of ways. Follow along with me for a moment. This exercise is a Deepak Chopra Center deep dive. I am going to ask you the question, "Who are you?" Take a moment to think of a response. What is your initial response? The first time I did this exercise my response was to answer according to the boxes I have been placed in within society. My response was, "I am a mother." "I am a daughter." "I am a job title." If you answered in a similar way, you are boxing yourself in. You are defining yourself by your outward roles in life which are impermanent.

You are so much more than your outward roles in this world. Take a moment to rethink your response to the question that you feel resonates from deep within your soul. Your answer will come from your heart, not your brain. Reflect on your subconscious, your true inner wild. This is the part of you inside that is constant. Here are some examples of responses that you may find easier to relate to:

I am a healer.
I am powerful.
I am a leader.
I am kindness.
I am a peacemaker.
I am caring.
I am happiness.
I am the universe.
I am compassion.
I am creative.
I am intelligence.
I am empathy.
I AM LOVE.

Now that you have a better understanding of the question, what is your response? How did your answer change? Never forget the beauty of who you truly are inside. You can now carry this inner knowing with you. You are so much more than a box. It's time to burn the box and let your inner wild light the match. The more we connect with our inner wild, the harder she will work for you. The mantra of "do less to attract more" requires us to let go of our false sense of control and trust our inner wild to make meaningful work happen for us. You have the power to re-wild the American Dream on your own terms.

Re-Wilding Your Own American Dream

The best thing you can ever do for yourself is to give yourself the gift of living your best life. Oprah reminds us, "The biggest adventure you can ever take is to live the life of your dreams." Now that we know the stereotypical version of the American Dream is a fallacy that allows the system to entrap our inner wild and fails us altogether, we have the power to re-wild the American Dream on our own terms. It is important, especially as women, that we re-wild our own version of the American Dream. By defining our own unique version of the American Dream, we effectively flee the ant farm and become the lone, rebel ant.

Whether you choose to change careers entirely, launch your own business or switch to a job description that better utilizes what makes you feel alive inside, our inner wild thrives when we choose to capitalize on our own unique talents. You don't need to quit your job today to re-wild. You can re-wild on your own terms and timeline. Even subtle acts of re-wilding at work can make a huge impact on our overall life satisfaction and wellbeing.

Re-wilding your American Dream begins with exploring your passion. What gives you that spark inside? You will never regret re-wilding your life around something you love. We all have something that we call our greatest passion in life. We are all really good at something that makes a positive difference in our lives and the lives of others. Your greatest passion is a part of your inner wild, the true you being your best self. No matter how much you may be balancing in your life as a busy adult woman, you can re-wild exactly where you are at. The journey of re-wilding simply opens you up to greater life satisfaction and positive change by tuning into your greatest passion. Your inner wild will guide you toward what makes you feel that spark inside.

If you are not sure what your passion is, that is ok. It may be that you have not had time to explore it yet. Take your time to look inside of yourself to discover it. One way to discover your passion is to look inside of yourself. Your greatest passion lies within your heart, not your head. Your greatest passion is something that you feel, not decide. Take a moment to reflect now on your now and Zen. Your now and Zen lights that spark inside of you. Your now and Zen may even be your greatest passion.

You can put your inner wild to work for you and capitalize from your greatest passion. Women are now turning their now and Zen passion into a profitable side gig or even their own business. Consider using your now and Zen passion projects in life to create a new career based entirely on what you enjoy doing. I started working as a consultant and within a few months I was writing full-time and working on meaningful projects with some of my favorite authors. I cannot even begin to express the gratitude and joy I feel having re-wilded my day job. Like my friend who quit her secure government job to move to Montana and start her own yoga and wellness center, I have another friend who created a business consulting firm for women entrepreneurs. I have another friend who has taken her love of silversmithing and started her own jewelry company in Arizona. Her unique, one-of-a-kind pieces sell out in minutes.

I have seen some of my closest friends who ride motorcycles turn their greatest passion, riding, into a career. They now work in the motorcycle industry as social media influencers, artists, marketing mavens and business developers. Surround yourself with fellow dreamers. Reaching out to other women who have inspired me has given me strength I never knew possible. I have friends who have been in the trenches working hard to make their own way in their lives. I find I get the best advice from them because they are going through the struggle. They are putting up the good fight to live the life of their dreams. I encourage you to reach out and network with women who inspire you! It is an incredible feeling to be a part of a sisterhood of women who take the risk for the reward of celebrating their inner wild by finding a way to live off their dreams. We are out here in droves, and we are wild as hell because we put no limits on the power of our inner wild to manifest our greatest dreams.

Failure is a Pebble

The saying, "Never give up on a dream just because of the time it will take. The time will pass anyway" is a strong reminder our dreams will never give up on us. We can transform our failures in life into positive experiences. Trust your inner wild. Your inner wild will kick failure's ass every time. At times in life when I need to choke down failures, I focus on the fact it is just a matter of time before I can accomplish my goals.

There is an Aesop's fable about the crow and the water pitcher. In summary, there is a thirsty crow who finds a pitcher with water at the bottom that he cannot reach. After trying repeatedly to reach the water and failing he begins to drop little pebbles into the pitcher, slowly raising up the water level to the point where he is finally rewarded with being able to drink the water. The crows' patience and refusal to give up on quenching his thirst eventually pays off.

As a first-generation college student, I dreamed of getting my doctorate degree. I was rejected by every Ph.D. program I applied for. I had earned a 4.0 grade point average during my first master's degree, and I won my department award for Best Thesis. Despite my solid academic work and feeling extremely confident, my dream of getting into a doctoral program was quickly shattered. I remember the excited anticipation I would feel when I would receive a letter in the mail from a program, I had applied for only to feel a deep sinking feeling in my gut from not being accepted. The competition for these programs is fierce. Everyone else applying to the same programs has similar academic achievements and test scores and thus Ph.D. programs choose their candidates based upon their research interests. Either you are a good research fit, or not. I clearly wasn't a good fit.

I took each of my rejection letters and hung them up to form my "wall of rejection." These rejections fueled my fire, especially when I saw others, I had graduated with give up on applying for other programs. I knew that it was just a matter of time and potentially more rejections until I found my place. I also knew I would never give up. Giving up on my dream of getting a doctorate degree would be a lifelong regret that I knew would haunt me. My ability to keep trying for my dream was bigger than my fear of rejection. The burden of giving up would have felt too awful to bear. I simply could not imagine my future without making my dream become a reality.

I was more afraid of losing my dream of furthering my education than rejection. Like the crow, I decided to take a chance and get creative. I called graduate programs and emailed individual professors around the country to see what their research interests were before I applied to their program. I wish I had done this in the first place, but it took my experience of being rejected again and again to learn the best strategy for applying. Eventually I met a professor at the College of Education at University of Wyoming who shared the same research interests I wanted to pursue. I applied to the newly formed Ph.D. program in Adult Learning and Postsecondary Education, and I was accepted. I was grateful I did not give up on myself and my dream.

I compare each of my rejection letters to the pebbles the crow uses to raise the water higher to each of the rejections we may receive in life. Today, if I had a wall of rejection letters from the amount of "dream" jobs I have applied for, they could fill a mansion. We hear so many reminders in life about the person who never gives up is the one that wins. There is so much truth to this statement. I have always found my place. Remember, your thoughts are powerful things and by perceiving continued rejections as pebbles towards progress rather than negative experiences, you are better to connect with your true life light and be motivated to let your inner wild come to life, no matter how much time it takes. The universe always comes through, especially when we refuse to give up. Don't be afraid to dream big!

Be Your Own Boss, Babe

Here is how your inner wild works. The more you connect with your truest desires and surrender your dreams to your truest intentions, the sooner your dreams or something even better happens. You do less to attract more. Sounds easy enough, right? Notice the phrase "surrender your dreams to your truest intentions". Your inner wild works like magic when we get out of our own way and stop trying to control every outcome in our lives.

Surrendering control is hard. We are taught to overwork ourselves to earn our dreams. Working hard is great! Hard work can be incredibly rewarding. It is when we overwork ourselves over an extended period of time, we begin to become a slave to the time clock and lose sight of utilizing your inner wild to attract what you want. We are going to explore the negative effects of overworking ourselves and how to stop doing it because it simply does not work. Overwork gives us a false sense of control. Overworking ourselves is an outdated concept. The notion of an 8 to 5 workday began during the Industrial Revolution in the 1800's, yet we are barely beginning to rethink this archaic work model.

The societal and cultural value of overworking ourselves came from pilgrims landing in America. Overworking ourselves is a Calvinistic, religious concept that has been ingrained in American and Western culture for hundreds of years. The idea is that by overworking yourself you can better control your outcomes in life. That makes sense if you are a pilgrim, and you need to work 24/7 to survive. In today's world, most of us are familiar with overworking ourselves. We are taught that if we overwork ourselves, we will be more successful, but this is not how success works. We gain success through hard work and attracting what we want to achieve, making control an illusion. The bottom line is we do not have control over anyone or anything outside of ourselves.

Overwork leads to burnout, not to mention it negatively affects our mental, spiritual, and physical health. Overworking yourself does not guarantee your dreams will come true. In fact, getting caught up in the guilt cycle of feeling you need to basically kill yourself to make your dreams come true works against the willingness of your inner wild to simply meet you where you are at. Overworking yourself does not equal success.

Overworking ourselves gets old, especially when we are doing work that does not take advantage of our innate talents. During my years of overworking myself I longed for the freedom I had in college where I had breaks in my schedule and was not being devoured by the meeting monster daily. I have an introvert side to me. I appreciate being with groups of people in doses, but I also value my quiet time. I prefer interpersonal workplace communication over meetings.

Being in meetings with groups of people all day literally drains the life right out of me. At the height of my former career life, I was at the office up to 12 hours per day and in meetings every one of those hours. I barely saw my daughter. I would come home exhausted and "peopled out". Over the years as I was promoted, the larger my office became the more meetings I was booked in. Through the first 15 years of my career, I managed thousands of employees. In between meetings I would have a line outside of my office door and hundreds of emails to go through after work each day. My inner wild was dead on arrival. Something had to change.

I re-wilded my career in small, meaningful ways that have transformed my entire work life in beautiful, meaningful ways. I now work in a way that capitalizes my inner wild. I am free from trying to force myself to do a job that does not light a spark inside of me. I began to tailor my career in a way that allowed me to feel a burning desire to wake up and go to work again. I realize my passion is to work on creative projects and not to sit in meetings all day. I also do not want to oversee a large staff as that comes with its own set of unique challenges.

By focusing on meaningful projects, I work solo in peace while nurturing productive relationships with my team. I work hard but no longer overwork myself. I have unlimited time off and I can choose to work at an office or at home. The most rewarding part of re-wilding my work is that I am now home to greet my daughter when she gets home from school. Re-wilding my work has brought me an incredible sense of freedom, joy, and motivation in my work. Being able to have the flexibility to be there for my daughter is priceless.

Perhaps I had to be pushed to my outer limits and begin to self-destruct before I realized I desperately needed to make changes in my work. For years I mistakenly thought overworking myself would not only numb my emotions and PTSD, but it would result in success. The result was I had a fancy job title and had lost all sense of wellbeing in my body, mind, and soul. The hardest part of doing less to attract more is letting go of our false sense of control. Once you understand how control does not serve you, you can harness your inner wild to guide you toward meaningful success in your life and work. You are ready to explore how to let your inner wild guide you toward doing less and attracting more good in your life by harnessing the power of intention.

Control v. Intention

Control is a fucking illusion. I can be a total control freak sometimes. Seriously, I am highly anal retentive and annoying and when it comes to planning I can drive my friends crazy. If you ever go on a motorcycle trip with me expect a full packing list and safety item checklist. I will ask you to bring everything from duct tape to tools to zip ties. I will meticulously map out our trip to take the most scenic route on backroads where the goal is to not see other cars for hours at a time. I will prepare us for the upcoming weather along the way. I will ask you how many gallons your gas tank holds so I can properly map out gas stops along the way.

I will advise you to wear layers and sunscreen and a helmet and to use bungee nets on top of your luggage to quickly pull over and put on a warmer leather jacket. I expect you to be prepared if you hit the road with me because beyond good preparation there is nothing else, we can control. Mother nature and fate can make us their Bish on a moment's notice. We cannot control the weather. We cannot control the road conditions. We cannot control our bikes suddenly breaking down. We cannot control cagers who stare at their cell phones while driving. We cannot control a deer suddenly jumping out in front of us on the road. I try and control the controllable factors and then fuck the rest. I let loose and have a great time!

Being the occasional control freak, I understand surrendering control is one of the hardest things we can do. Trust me when I tell you surrendering control is worth the reward! We are taught to overwork ourselves to earn our dreams. Overwork gives us a false sense of control over the fate of our career. Here is the truth about overworking ourselves. The concept of overworking ourselves came over on the boat when pilgrims settled in the U.S. It is a Calvinistic, religious concept that has been ingrained in American and Western culture for hundreds of years.

It is much easier to surrender control and trust our inner wild once we realize control is an illusion. Harnessing the power of your inner wild begins with realizing re-wilding is not about control, especially since we have no control outside of ourselves. All we can do is our best and surrender our false sense of control. You can trust your inner wild to have your back. Whereas intuition is the voice of your inner wild, intention is the manifesting power of your inner wild. Intention is the part of your inner wild that makes shit happen, but you need to release control to allow this magic to unfold. The key to tapping directly into your inner wild to manifest good things in your life comes from understanding and aligning with the immense power of your intention.

So, what is intention? Dr. Wayne W. Dyer explains:

> It's the difference between motivation and inspiration. Motivation is when you get hold of an idea and don't let go of it until you make it a reality. Inspiration is the reverse—when an idea gets hold of you and you feel compelled to let that impulse or energy carry you along. You get to a point where you realize that you're no longer in charge, that there's a driving force inside you that can't be stopped. Look at the great athletes, musician, artists, and writers. They all tap into a source.
>
> He then goes on to explain, "Intention is not something you do, but rather a force that exists in the universe as an invisible field of energy—a power that can carry us." Intention does not make mistakes. Intention is in our very nature. A seed will grow into what it is meant to be. A caterpillar emerges from its cocoon

a butterfly. Your intention is far more powerful than the American Dream. Like the CEO's mentioned earlier who created multi-million-dollar companies from following their burning desire to manifest their greatest dreams, they all had powerful intentions that far outweighed all the obstacles in their path. They surpassed the American Dream when they released their intention to create mega successful companies, they believed in with all their hearts, minds, and souls.

    The beauty of accessing the power of your intention relieves you of feeling you must do all the work. You literally do less and attract all the good and better into your life and work. Dr. Wayne Dyer recommends the fastest way to tap into intention is to remind yourself of these five words, I want to feel good! Rather than tell yourself, "I have to….." try using these five words instead. Like an athlete visualizing the feeling of winning, focus on what makes you feel good. We know that when we feel good, we attract all the good in the universe our way. There is no reason to overwork yourself to make your dreams come true, and the best news is you don't have to! It is healthier for your mind, body, and soul to do less and attract more abundance and success in your life. If at first the thought of trusting the universe sounds "woo woo" and "out there" stick with me and keep reading because this stuff really works. Your mindset defines how you see your world and your place in it. If you see your world as giving and abundant, you will likely be surrounded by or create new opportunities that match your inner wild. No dream is too big. We cannot accomplish our dreams until we have the power to dream them in the first place. Remember, you attract what you are, not what you want.

Defining Your Universe

    There is an old folktale a friend told me while backpacking solo through China that really hit home in regard to how the universe brings us exactly what we are. A traveler came upon an old man sitting on a rock beside the road. The traveler asked the old man, "What sort of people live in the next town?" Answering his question with his own question the old man asked the traveler, "What were the people like where you've come from?" The traveler replied, "The people where I come from are bad. They lie and steal and cheat. They are the most selfish people in the world, and they cannot be trusted. I am happy to never see them again." The old man answered, "Is that right? Well, I'm sorry to say that the people in the next town are the same." Feeling let down, the traveler went on his way to the village and the old man continued to relax on his rock.

Later that day another traveler asked the old man the same question, "What sort of people live in the next town?" Answering his question with his own question the old man asked the traveler, "What were the people like where you've come from?" The traveler replied, "They are the best people I have ever known. They are honest, friendly, and kind. I am sorry to not see them again." The old man answered, "Is that right? Well, I'm happy to say that the people in the next town are the same." Feeling excited, the traveler went on his way to the village and the old man continued to relax on his rock.

The traveler's tale reinforces the fact that wherever you go, there you are. The intention you put out into this world; you get back. I have read all the books written by the late internationally renowned author and speaker in the field of self-development, Dr. Wayne W. Dyer. He has had a profound impact on my life by teaching me to trust the universe when it comes to manifesting my inner wild and greatest dreams. Dr. Dyer explains, "One of the most important decisions you'll ever make is choosing the kind of universe you exist in." He also said, "You don't get what you want. You get what you are."

Universal Spaghetti

One of the most beautiful things about intention is it allows you to work with your power of creativity. I refer to the creation process with my coworkers, or co captains as I prefer to refer to them, as throwing spaghetti at the wall to see what sticks. We brainstorm ideas and keep what sticks. The sticky spaghetti ideas inspire us and define our mojo moving forward in creating programs that can help change people's lives. A few weeks ago, I sent out emails to business partners with Universal Spaghetti in the subject line. I was writing to let them know my intentions of putting this book out into the universe and to let them know I'd love to collaborate. That's it. There was not a clear request nor plan. I just let them know they may be a part of an upcoming universal plan. Putting your intentions out to the universe is like throwing spaghetti at the wall to see what sticks. My universal spaghetti co captains are the people I share my intentions with. They are also dreamers who understand and trust in the universe, so they get it.

I am careful to share my intentions and dreams only with those close to me who understand the power of the universe to make shit happen. I have learned from experience that when I share my intentions with someone who is not capable of understanding my intentions, they challenge the worth of my dream and negate my ability to make it happen. Don't expect someone to understand or support your intentions when they may not share your vision.

Other people may not understand your dreams and that's ok. Their comments can be destructive to your dreams. Don't let what others think of your dreams hold you back. Give yourself permission to re-wild and live a life most people don't understand. You're worth it & those who love you also deserve to see you thrive & be happy. Keep your eyes on the stars and your dreams close to your heart.

Let's get to work on aligning your intentions with the universe so you can do less and attract more. Please take a moment to read the following affirmations as many times as you need to:

I am [insert your response to the question "Who am I?" you reflected on earlier in this chapter].

"I have the power to connect with my inner wild to manifest my best life on my own terms to feel greater purpose, happiness and success everyday."

I don't chase, I attract.

I choose to re-wild on my own terms.

When I feel overwhelmed, I choose to take the time I need to recharge.

When I feel good, I set my intentions for all things good or better.

I am connected to the endless abundance of my inner wild.

I am a magnet attracting everything that brings the highest good.

I trust my inner wild with my intentions to make my greatest dreams or better happen.

Self-Reflection Exercise: Your Greatest Dreams

Let's begin putting your greatest hopes and dreams out into the universe!

Congratulations on making it to this point. You are doing important work. Each moment you take to write about the life of your dreams you automatically start to put it out to the universe. Allow yourself time to dig deep and reflect on the following questions. I encourage you to write out your responses in your re-wilding journal.

Take time to reflect on the following questions:

- If money was no object and you never had to work another day in your life, what would you want to do?
- What are your greatest hopes and dreams?
- What is it about your dreams that makes you feel good inside of your heart and soul?
- If you get to live a long life where all your dreams, or better, come true, how do you want to be remembered?

I encourage you to journal your passion and dreams. Reflect on how your dreams make you feel good inside. This feeling is your connection with your inner wild shining brightly. It is powerful. You can use that good feeling to attract more good in your life. What may seem like a small act of connecting with your inner wild, becomes a powerful intention you can fully manifest into your daily reality. Even if you don't fully trust your inner wild to deliver yet, keep dreaming!

Chapter 11: Your Future Wild

"The new dawn blooms as we free it. For there is always light, if only we are brave enough to see it. If only we're brave enough to be it."
Amanda Gorman

How many times have we heard the saying, "the only thing constant in life is change," yet, when change happens, especially when it happens instantly, it can leave you feeling stranded on a desert island completely alone in a rainstorm with lightning flashing all around you. We all face moments in our life that leave us changed forever. When the Covid-19 pandemic arrived, it turned our world upside down. Many of us suffered unspeakable loss. Many of us are still recovering from losing someone we love to Covid. Many of us got laid off and are struggling to get back on our feet. Even in the absolute deepest moments of despair you can rely on your inner wild to love you, support you, and help you navigate the dark moments we must face in this beautiful thing we call life. Your inner wild is your best life raft.

I put off writing this book for over a year because covid showed up and kicked my ass. Around the time I planned to start writing this book, the world shut down and suddenly we found ourselves living in the Covid-19 pandemic, quarantined at home. For some reason covid really, really loves me. What I now refer to as "the Vid", Covid-19 is like a bad stalker that refuses to give up. I now live with long-haul Covid. I lost all sense of taste for six months. A huge part of my work is presenting. I lost my voice. I had a raspy voice for over a year. My sense of smell is still distorted. Perfumes make me gag. They smell like burned garlic to me. I still experience extreme fatigue. Naps are my BFF. The worst part of long-haul Covid for me has been the daily struggle to breathe as my lungs are still mysteriously inflamed. I have tried every treatment recommended from herbs to acupuncture to IV therapy. Nothing worked. I now rely on a steroid inhaler every day to help me function.

One month after I got the Vid, which left me tired enough, I became even more exhausted. My mind was so foggy it was a struggle to concentrate. I did not feel comfortable driving because I was so groggy, I backed my vehicle into a highly obvious brick wall I would have never hit otherwise. It turns out my immune system was so compromised from the Vid I ended up with Mononucleosis, also known as the teenage kissing disease. I wish I had done something fun to get it, but unfortunately there is no exciting story behind how I got it.

Mono is nothing short of living in a debilitating fog. My body ached for months. During my Zoom meetings I was in pain as I could not sit up for more than ten minutes without my back aching. I don't remember much from the time I had mono. I was told I was sleeping around 18 hours per day for about three months. During the hours I was awake and could focus I would use that time to finish my work, then I would sleep. I would literally wake up and type and then crash again in bed with my laptop. Thankfully my daughter never got Covid from me and I was able to recover from home snuggled up with my dogs.

During the many months I was exhausted from Covid-19 and Mono, when cabin fever got the best of me, I tried to ride my motorcycle a few times. I ended up dropping my bike twice. I no longer had the strength to hold her up safely. I could no longer ride my motorcycle. We lived in Texas at the time and riding in the Texas heat left me feeling spent and beyond exhausted. Once I even attempted to hit the road again like I used to. I planned to ride from Texas to Phoenix to meet friends for Arizona Bike Week. I made it to El Paso, and I was exhausted. I was so disoriented I lost my wallet.

I ended up staying in a hotel to recover. Luckily, we found my wallet in the bushes near where I had parked my bike. At this point I canceled the rest of my trip and had the most hot, exhausting ride back through the West Texas desert I had ever experienced on my motorcycle. And this is saying a lot! If you have ever ridden back from Sturgis after a week of having an incredible time, sitting in the hot sun all day for days on end and barely sleeping it can only compare to a wild trip to Las Vegas. My ride home that day was long and hot and far worse than a hungover ride back from Sturgis. When I got my bike back home and put my kickstand down in the garage, I realized I no longer had the desire to ride. My passion to ride was gone. I lost my now and zen.

Get Lost in the Right Direction

It feels good to get lost in the right direction. Prior to getting the Vid, road tripping on my Harley-Davidson motorcycle has always been my greatest go-to therapy. It took nearly a year and a half for me to feel healthy enough to ride my motorcycle again. Long-haul Covid is a mysterious thing. Over the course of just a few days I suddenly found myself able to breathe without my inhaler. My energy suddenly returned. This was not a slow change. It happened almost overnight. I was feeling 75% of my old self again.

The moment I woke up and could take a full breath without my inhaler, I immediately dropped everything and mapped out a 3,000-mile motorcycle trip from Denver through Arizona and on to California to meet a badass group of fellow women riders at Babes Ride Out in the southern California desert. I was nervous to ride again since I was not able to handle my motorcycle for so long. I had lost my love of riding and I needed this road trip to know if my Harley Diamondson days were over or not.

It was long overdue I connected with my freedom machine and spent time with the most amazing women on earth. Stay tuned because little did I know at the time, I would fall in love again before my journey was over. When it comes to riding a motorcycle, you don't have to be rich to have an amazing travel experience. A tank of motorcycle gas costs less than 15 bucks and can take you over 200 miles. I wanted to ride through states and on roads I have never seen before. Rather than let my fear stop me, I let my inner wild take over and I packed for my journey.

My first day of my trip I rode solo from Denver, Colorado to Moab, Utah. I arrived in Moab in October at the height of jeep season and when I pulled into a main street gas station I had yet to find a hotel for the night. As I began to make calls to try and find a room for the night, I quickly realized I should have made plans ahead of time. I tossed aside my usual modus operandi of planning every detail of my moto trip and I didn't make reservations in Moab. While I was calling for hotels I had about ten random people ask if they could see my bike up close and take pictures. My Harley Diamondson is always a great conversation piece. The way the gas station lights were glinting off her that night reminded me of just how beautiful she is and how much I missed her. I met people visiting Moab from all over the world that night. I eventually found a room and crashed for the evening.

My goal for the next day was to ride through Monument Valley on the border of Utah and Arizona. You may remember Monument Valley as the backdrop for the scene in Forrest Gump where he finally stops running. You can Google Forrest Gump Hill to navigate to the most perfect view of Monument Valley. It is breathtaking. I wanted to go there for years and when I put my kickstand down it was a perfect, bright, and sunny day. You remember how I mentioned your vibe attracts your tribe?

While I was there, I met the creators and owners of a motorcycle inspirational lifestyle motorcycle clothing company of which I am a big fan. They are from Wyoming (shout out!) and chose to stay home and form a thriving company in our home state. When they saw my bike parked on the side of the road they decided to pull over and check out the Harley Diamondson. The fact we ended up at Monument Valley on the same day, at the same time, and talked about motorcycles was truly a serendipitous moment. I knew my inner wild had landed me right where I needed to be.

Over the next week I rode through Arizona. I took a tour of Antelope Canyon on the Navajo Nation. It was an amazing experience. You must have a native Navajo tour guide take you through the slot canyon. Our tour guide shared so many interesting facts about the land and his culture. I learned that day to refer to the Navajo Nation in their native language as Dine (din-eh). I stopped by the Cameron Trading Post where they specialize in selling certified, handmade, finely crafted jewelry. Indian gemologists describe black onyx as a symbol of protection for harmonious relationships. I felt compelled to buy a large black oval-shaped onyx ring for my wedding ring finger. The moment I saw it, I knew I had to have it and it fit perfectly.

After touring the Dine Nation, I stayed at a beautiful boutique hotel where I spoiled myself in Sedona. I fell in love with Sedona and the energy there so much I might move there someday. From Sedona I rode south to Tucson. I got caught in a huge monsoon rainstorm south of Phoenix and hid under a bridge like a troll as I watched up to six inches of water accumulate around my bike. It was so hot I let myself get soaking wet in the rain and chose not to put on my rain gear.

Storms always end on the road, just like they do in life. Once the rain subsided, I hit the road again, cooled off and refreshed. The wind dried me off in just a few minutes. I stayed in Tucson for a few days and attended a work conference. I had packed my gorgeous emerald green silk jumpsuit and high heels in my bike luggage for the business portion of my trip. When I rolled up to the Ventana Canyon Resort I looked like I had been ridden hard and put away wet, and technically I was, but I loved the ride on the way, storms, and all.

Babes Ride Out

My next stop was Babes Ride Out in Borrego Springs, California. I was heading to the southern California desert to meet a friend I had met only briefly but we shared positive energy and vibes together. We both dream of having an alpaca ranch someday. Need I say more? She invited me to join her tribe of best friends on their trip together. I didn't know any of these other women. But I do know this. When you are a woman and you ride a motorcycle, you are an automatic member of the wild wind club. You instantly become a member of an extremely powerful, bonded sisterhood. I am so grateful these women all welcomed me. We are inextricably connected by our inner wild.

We rode through the desert together for a few hundred miles. We laughed together. We partied together. We camped out under the southern California desert sky. These women are my tribe. We all are instantly bonded by our shared love of the freedom and excitement riding gives us. We rode around the southern California desert, the Salton Sea and visited Resurrection Mountain. We stayed up late and had a blast with the other women who had come from around the country and Mexico for the event.

    I had a long ride home and by the time I hit the Rocky Mountains I had left the high temperature of the southern Arizona desert behind. I was riding in 30-degree weather across the mountains along I-70 to Denver. I was prepared but when you ride in the cold you also need to calculate the wind you are up against as it seriously drops the temperature even further. It was a frosty ride and my bike kept stalling in the mountains. My bike gave out and stalled at the top of Vail Pass in Colorado around 10,662 feet above sea level, but I limped my worn-out bike home safely, exhausted, exhilarated and my heart was completely full.

    I fell in love with riding my motorcycle all over again on this trip. It felt exhilarating to reconnect with my greatest love. The moment we first touched after so much time had gone by, I felt a huge wave of nervousness and excitement rush over me. I felt my breath caught in my throat and had to concentrate to breathe. I closed my eyes and fully inhaled the excitement of each moment we spent together. I inhaled her familiar scent of gasoline and oil. I had thought our time together in this life may have been over forever. I was wrong. We returned to our instant connection the moment we hit a few hundred miles together. I had butterflies in my stomach each time I started her engine. We spent hours and thousands of miles together reminiscing. I shared my deepest feelings and thoughts with her. I cried in my helmet, and she listened like a best friend. I shared my future hopes and dreams. We daydreamed together for days as we rode together through the forest, desert, vineyards, and Rocky Mountains. I have never had a love like this in my life. This is me falling back in love with my motorcycle. My one true love. I am my full inner wild with my motorcycle. We are one.

Re-Wild Your Own Fortune

The moment I got home I was road weary from riding my bike as it was breaking down. I was chilled to the bone from my freezing motorcycle ride through Vail Pass and the Rockies. My fingertips and toes were completely numb. I can wear warmer gear on my hands and feet, but I choose not to. I don't like the bulk and extra heating wires I need to plug into my battery required for heated gloves and socks while I ride so I tough it out. As I was peeling off my layers of leather in the middle of my kitchen the feeling of warmth slowly began to creep back into my body.

Right before my road trip I had ordered a few things from Go Fast, Don't Die, the motorcycle company based in Wyoming whose creators and owners I had just met in Monument Valley. I find it so ironic and humorous the entire time I lived and worked in China I never saw one fortune cookie. However, my order from Wyoming had arrived complete with a random fortune cookie. I stopped reading fortune cookies years ago because of the mass manufactured messages seem more obtuse than entertaining. This fortune cookie was different. Its message was so unique that once I read it, I put it up on my refrigerator as a daily reminder.

While thawing out from my savage ride home from Babes Ride Out, I looked over and read the message and was reminded of how everything from my motorcycle journey fit together so beautifully. The fortune cookie message reads:

"Other side is blank. Write your own fortune."

Time to Re-Wild

"She remembered who she was and the game changed." - Lalah Deliah

This may be the end of our time together for now, but it is just the beginning of your re-wilding journey. Please remember your inner wild will never fail you. She is powerful because she is undeniably the true YOU. She is also here to constantly remind you of your greatest purpose in this life so you can live the life of your dreams. You deserve to experience the positive psychological, spiritual, and physical wellbeing and enhanced success in all you do that comes from being one with your inner wild. May you re-wild in happiness!

Here is my wish for you. May you "misbehave" in the most GLORIOUS ways! Do brave things. Reap in the joy you deserve to feel in your life. May you now look self-doubt and fear in the face and confidently tell her to fuck off and be gone. Be wild and free. You were born ready to write your own story. It is time for you to go forth, re-wild and live the life of your dreams!
May we meet in the wind someday.

Epilogue

My gratitude list is overflowing when it comes to the support I received while writing this book. Someone once told me "Writing is all about re-writing" and they were right. Writing a book is a massive undertaking. I could not have done this without the support I have had from those of you crazy enough to love me and support me along the way.

Without hesitation I dedicate this book to all the women out there who are struggling to live the life of their dreams they deserve. May you re-wild in glorious ways! I am thankful for YOU, the reader. This book cannot exist without each of you. Thank you for trusting me to take you on this wild journey. Thank you for putting up with my smart-ass sense of humor and potty mouth.

Please write to me and share your stories of re-wilding. I cannot wait to hear about you living your best life on your own wild terms! Namaste and God Bless.

I dedicate this book to my daughter, the light of my life and amateur comedian. We started this journey together. You helped me make sense of my occasional writing blocks. Since the day you came into my life you have given me a sense of motivation and inspiration of unbounded proportions. I am so lucky I have been given the gift of being your mother. I hope the sacrifices along the way allow you, my wonderful little one, to reap amazing rewards in this beautiful thing we call LIFE! May you continue to smile and shine as you do each day.

I thank my mom and dad. Mom, thank you for your endless words of encouragement. You are my rock. I still miss sitting on your lap like when I was a little kid! Ha-ha. Thank you for loving me no matter what! Dad, thank you for coming to me in my dreams when I need you the most. You are the best guardian angel ever. I am a part of each of you and you have influenced me in incredible ways. I dedicate this book to my work-husband of many years, Bill Bryan. May you R.I.P. I miss you every day. Thank you for your never-ending kindness. Although I never expected you to, thank you for never leaving work until I left first. You always made sure I made it through each day. Thank you for volunteering to drag my body out to the sidewalk if I started to kick the bucket at work.

    I thank my closest badass babes. You know who you are. You are so wild and cannot be contained and I love you for it. You exemplify what it is like to be true to ourselves and re-wild. Thank you for believing in me even when I didn't believe in myself.

    Thank you to my dear wind sister tribe. You are so wild and amazing, and I love all of your wind chapped asses! I am grateful to all of those who have helped me edit. Thank you for your brutal honesty and calling me out on my bullshit.

And finally, I dedicate this book to my one true love, my Harley Diamondson in an oddly phallic poem:

Motorcycle Now & Zen
Your wild vibe
Between my thighs
Hot skin baking under the sun one day
Frozen fingertips the next
Feeling the rush of the wind
Like a sweet kiss upon my lips

Each time I ride you
I get that undeniable rush
That reminds me we are one
You are not only my one true love
You are my forever crush

I hate to think of how tame life was before we met
It was not nearly so beautiful
As the way we now fit perfectly together
Dancing on high mountain twisties
As the storms we've ridden through
Dewy mornings riding by fragrant fields of spring wildflowers

When I die
I hope it's with you!
To know we lived the fullest life
And move on together
To more wild adventures in the next life too...

About the Author

Dr. Aimee, Ed.D., is a Wild Womxn Guide, Writer, Teacher and Speaker. She is the founder of the Wild Womxn Collective where she regularly conducts spiritual Re-Wilding workshops. She is passionate about helping women rediscover their wild woman within.

Raised in Green River, Wyoming, Aimee is a true Rocky Mountain girl.

A citizen of the world, she currently resides in Denver with her wild and wonderful teenager. Aimee has a gypsy heart and an insatiable case of travel and adventure lust. In her free time, she rides her Harley-Diamondson bedazzled with Swarovski crystals with her wind sisterhood of fellow wild women and loves to walk her dachshund in the park.

For more on Aimee visit DrAimeeCallahan.com

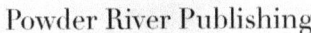

www.ingramcontent.com/pod-product-compliance
Ingram Content Group UK Ltd.
Pitfield, Milton Keynes, MK11 3LW, UK
UKHW021326180426
11947UKWH00017B/1468